Robert Hayward

A Merry Christmas

from

Aunt Jennie –

1906 –

AMERICAN TRAITS

FROM THE POINT OF VIEW
OF A GERMAN

BY

HUGO MÜNSTERBERG

BOSTON AND NEW YORK
HOUGHTON, MIFFLIN AND COMPANY
The Riverside Press, Cambridge

Published November, 1901

NINTH IMPRESSION

To

FREDERICK WILLIAM HOLLS

Member of the Permanent Court of Arbitration at the Hague

IDEAL TYPE OF THE

AMERICAN OF GERMAN DESCENT

PREFACE

THE following essays are not scholarly studies, but light sketches drawn in leisure hours by a German who has pitched his tent among the Americans and become interested in the differences between the Americans and the Germans. But my interest in that contrast is not merely a theoretical one : I believe that these two nations can and ought to learn from each other, and that in this case even the protectionists of national civilization ought not to favor a prohibitive tariff on foreign ideals. Such mutual instruction has been hindered by prejudices and misunderstandings : the two nations do not know each other sufficiently, although they are connected by innumerable ties from the past and will need each other's good will still more in the years to come. To root out such prejudices and to facilitate mutual benefit, it becomes a duty to measure critically the culture of the one country by the ideals of the other.

In this small volume the topic is discussed only
from one side, for this book is written for Americans, and for Americans only. The problem is,
therefore, not what Germany ought to learn from
the United States, but rather, how far a fuller
understanding of German ideals can be service-
able to American culture. Of course this point
of view has limited from the beginning the circle
of problems to demand consideration; thus it has
not been necessary to speak of commerce and industry and a hundred other topics with regard to
which Germans and Americans might be compared. And the choice of subjects has been further influenced by factors in the life of the author.
Schoolboy, student, and later university professor
in Germany, and now for seven years a professor
in America, I have been of course more closely in
contact with certain sides of civilization than with
others; it is thus natural that the problems of
education and scholarship take somewhat the central place in my discussions. Even the special
seat of observation must have had its influence on
my impressions: I was hardly surprised to read
the other day that I see the American world

through German eyes with Harvard astigmatism.

That I see it with German eyes is certainly true : it is the only reason which gives, perhaps, to these small sketches a right to exist ; if I saw America with the eyes of an American I should hardly hope to notice features which possibly my neighbors overlook. It is the contrast which brings out the lines, and that fact alone excuses my speaking to Americans on American subjects after so short a period of acquaintance; had I waited longer I should have seen my surroundings more nearly with American eyes and should have perceived less the characteristic differences. I think I can say at least that I have made the best use of these years of American life to come in contact with its infinite variety. While the Harvard life in Boston offers in itself a good opportunity to meet men and to feel the pulse of American civilization, I have traveled again and again over the country and have tried to experience the national life in all its important or characteristic phases.

These informal pages, of course, cannot show

wholly what American life has meant to me, inasmuch as my topic forces me to the side of the op-
position. If it is my aim to point to those features
of American life on which a comment in the light
of European ideals seems allowable, the picture
which I draw must appear one-sided, as the task
gives me no chance to linger on the superiorities
of American culture which do not need the re-
touching by foreign ideals. I am thus obliged to
put in all the shadows and to brush out the lights ;
therefore no one ought to imagine that it has
been my intention to draw a complete picture of
American life as it appears to me.

This preponderance of adverse criticism brings
an unavoidable result : I must express opinions
which are antagonistic to widely favored opinions
of the day, to pet theories, and to flourishing
customs. I have already experienced the consequences. All the five essays have appeared previously, the first three in the " Atlantic Monthly,"
the last two in the " International Monthly," —
I reprint them with the kind permission of the
magazines, — and their isolated appearance has
every time given rise to a public discussion of

unexpected vehemence. Especially the paper on education, which I had published under the title of "School Reform," brought forward ever new rejoinders which often indicated that I had touched a sore point. I have finally decided nevertheless to reprint all the papers with but slight alterations; I felt that my papers would become valueless if I ever shaded them for the purpose of escaping antagonism. And further, if I look backward I cannot forget how much larger was the number of those who encouraged me to stand for my side of the case, and who insisted that it was the right time to raise a voice against the tendencies of the day.

Only one criticism has appeared in those utterances which seems to have weight, or at least seems certainly to be in order. It has been often questioned whether I am right in fighting merely against American shortcomings from a German point of view, and in trying to destroy prejudices on this side of the water; whether it is not in a still higher degree my duty to attempt the same for the other side; for German prejudices concerning the United States are certainly not less severe and the points in which Germany might learn from American culture not less numerous. The question is fair, and I should acknowledge its force had only my critics first made sure that I am not doing exactly what they urge. I have done it unceasingly and with my best energies ever since I came here : I have published on the other side scores of articles and essays, and shall soon put before the German public an entire book on American life, a book which is far less fragmentary than this, and deals in a detailed way with the political, economic, intellectual, and social aspects of American culture. Its purpose is to illuminate and to defend a culture which I have learned to admire and which is so greatly misunderstood over there; it seeks to interpret systematically the democratic ideals of America. It will be written for Germans only.

I know this method of double entry exposes me to the possibility, when detached paragraphs of my German essays are brought over here and published in translation, of seeming inconsistent or even insincere. And yet contradictions exist merely for the superficial observer; both statements express equally a sincere conviction. A little strip of gray paper appears white on a black background and black on a white one; so my statements can express the same truth on both sides only if the peculiarities of public opinion they encounter are considered beforehand. What I write in Germany to counteract the prejudices against America would sound on American soil like cheap flattery, and would be not only useless, but would stand in the way of reform; on the other hand, that which I publish here would sound there like utter condemnation, it would reinforce unfriendly opinions, and would be in fact misleading, since it would be exaggerated by the existing prejudices and would not be supplemented by a knowledge of the really salient high lights. The wrong would thus be done not by the author who emphasizes the good points of America over there, and criticises the weak ones here, but by those who detach such studies from their background.

My last word is, therefore, a serious request that no one, especially no German-American who agrees with me as to the need of good relations between the two countries, should quote or translate from this little book in a German paper over in the fatherland. So far as I can help it, no copy of the book shall reach the European continent; and I can promise in return also to take pains when I publish my German book on America that none of the amiabilities I may have to promulgate over there shall recross the ocean and dull my criticism here.

HUGO MÜNSTERBERG.

CAMBRIDGE, MASS., October, 1901.

CONTENTS

AMERICAN TRAITS

I

THE AMERICANS AND THE GERMANS

I

During the last years, and especially since the beginning of the Spanish war, scarcely a month has passed which has not brought to public notice some fancied friction between the Americans and the Germans, and again and again the scareheads of sensational newspapers have suggested the possibility of a clash. Since England is no longer a bogy to frighten the Americans, the Germans have to be the target of all the suspicion and bad feeling which some Americans like to cultivate against Europe, a feeling always encouraged by those politicians who want to bolster up new schemes by vague allusions to a threatening danger beyond the sea. Whether Captain Coghlan or an agrarian in the fatherland has talked inconsiderately, whether Dewey and Diedrichs or Chaffee and Waldersee are the actors, whether Samoa or China, the West Indies or Brazil is in question, whether meat inspection and the importation of American apples or a tariff change on this side is under discussion, whether in Congress or the Reichstag the industrial development of the future is forecast, the facts are each time pointed out to us as dangerous clouds whose lightnings may strike us before the next newspaper edition. All this, however, is politics; whether serious conflicts were really impending or not, why should a student of social psychology concern himself with the situation?

But may we not be deceiving ourselves if we think that the real trouble has been in Manila or Apia or Pekin, or that it will ever take its rise in the market places of the world where American and German industry are in competition? Is it not rather the mental state of the two nations that is the only possible source of any danger? The object of quarrel is insignificant; it is the inner attitude which counts. If Americans and Germans like one another and have sympathy for one another's character, the whole of China will be too small to cause a conflict; but if there is an antipathy between them, if neither trusts the nature of the other, the tiniest rock in the ocean may suffice to bring on a war which shall set the globe ablaze. Does not all this give an excuse to the psychologist who, though far from the mysteries of politics, ventures to take an impartial view of this interesting emotional case?

To live up to all the opportunities of scholarly display which this chapter of social psychology offers, I ought to go back to the seventeenth century or at least to Frederick the Great, whose enthusiasm for the American struggle for independence furnishes plenty of material for all who like to make such introductions. But I am afraid that the usual fine quotations which show the absence of American-German frictions in earlier times have hardly any direct bearing on our present case. The Germans of a generation ago did not look much beyond the ocean in any case, and the German imagination pictured the land rather than the nation, — the land where gold was lying in the streets, and where every newcomer still found the chance of a free life. The American as a special type of man had not been discovered; neither favorable nor unfavorable information about him was diffused, simply because nobody asked for it. On the American side it was somewhat different. Millions of German immigrants had poured into the land, and had become an honest and most industrious part of the population. Moreover, while they were bringing the spirit of the German working classes, thousands of young Americans were going abroad to bring home the

spirit of educated Germany.   German music and
German philosophy, German joyousness and German university spirit, came to these shores ; and
yet, just as the American land of gold and liberty
remained to the imagination of the German something far and strange, so the Teutonic land of
thinkers and poets remained to the American imagination remote and vague.   No one thought of
comparison or of rivalry, because the two worlds
seemed in different dimensions.

But all this has changed overnight : the dreamy
German and the adventurous American are sitting
close together on the same bench, feeling that
they must be either friends or foes.   Wonderfully
as the cables and twin-screw steamers have diminished the distance in space between the two peoples, the diminution of the inner mental distance
has been still more surprising and unexpected
on both sides.   Germany has become strong,
rich, and powerful, and its politics have turned
into realistic paths.   On the other hand, the
United States, since the country has come to maturity economically, has put its gigantic resources
into the service of education and art and science.   They are both thus moving in the same
sphere, and the question is merely, Will they
move shoulder to shoulder, or be ever at vari-
ance ?   Their feelings and emotions, even their

moods, will decide about that : how do they feel
to-day ?

No sincere observer can deny that the two peoples in some respects do not like each other. It
is by no means hate nor even animosity which
separates them ; it is a kind of antipathy, a half-
ethical, half-æsthetic aversion. It would be superficial and wrong to deny this feeling, and to maintain that their dislike means commercial rivalry ;
both are too fair and broad-minded — indeed, I
may say, too idealistic — to dislike each other on
account of wheat and sugar and pork ; they might
struggle about the tariff, but tariff struggles become noisy and undignified affairs only because
the masses lack mutual respect. Neither Germans
nor Americans are accustomed in their social life
to treat the neighbor who happens to be a fair
competitor as an enemy. Competition is to them
a stimulant, but not a poison which paralyzes the
good will. The nations feel, like private citizens,
that the respect cannot be hurt by a divergence
of economic interests, and that even friendship is
possible in spite of emulation. But even those
who accept unhesitatingly the materialistic theory
of history, according to which economic factors
alone determine the development of human relations, have no case here, as in all essentials the
past relation of the two countries has been one of

mutual economic help, the one nation needing just that which the other supplied, and thus offering all the conditions for a solid union ; only the predictions of the future speak of rivalry, and they can certainly not account for the popular lack of sympathy in the past. The sharpness and unfriendliness of speech which is remarked sometimes on both sides in political and commercial matters is not the cause of the national attitude, but its effect. It is not an objective irritating situation which forces on the two peoples an angry emotion ; it is the underlying emotion which too easily gives to every indifferent situation a touch of antagonism. The feeling is the primary factor, and its source is a certain misapprehension of character. The citizens of the two nations do not like one another because they do not regard one another as gentlemen : the American thinks the German servile and reactionary, narrow-minded and narrow-hearted ; the German thinks the American greedy and vulgar, brutal and corrupt. As long as large circles of the population have such a feeling, all the diplomacy of the two governments can merely apply plaster to the wounds, but cannot thoroughly heal them. Only one course is open for an organic improvement : the two nations must learn to understand each other and to feel the inner accord of their real characters.

II

Caricatures are not portraits, but they can be helpful in recognizing the essential features which the designer really believes himself to see in the original. The caricature of the German, popular from the Atlantic to the Pacific, is moreover not confined to the comic papers, but is excellently represented in the serious editorials of many newspapers ; and the funny German in a second-class American theatre is much less amusing than that absurd creature which in parlor gossip and club talk is quite seriously substituted for the inhabitant of the fatherland. An American who has never been abroad invited me, the other day, to a German luncheon. I had to work my way through a series of so-called German dishes, which I had never tasted or smelled before ; and when finally imported sauerkraut appeared, and I had to confess that I had never tried it in my life and had never seen any one else eating it, my host assured me that I did not know anything about Germany : it was the favorite dish of every Prussian. The habits of this Prussian sauerkraut-eater are well known. He goes shabbily dressed, never takes a bath, drinks beer at his breakfast, plays skat, smokes a long pipe, wears spectacles, reads books from dirty loan libraries, is rude to the lower classes and slavishly servile to the higher, is innocent of the slightest attempt at good form in society, considering it as his object in life to obey the policeman, to fill blanks with bureaucratic red tape, and to get a title in front of his name. Most of this genus fill their time with training parade step in the barrack courts; the others either make bad lyrical poems or live immoral lives, or sit in prison on account of daring to say a free word in politics. But their chief characteristic comes out in their relations to women and to the government. With calculating cruelty, they force women to remain uneducated and without rights; in marriage they treat them like silly playthings or servant-girls; a woman with intellectual or æsthetic interests is, like everything which suggests progress, a horror to their minds. And lastly, their government: it is hard to understand why, but it is a fact that they insist on living without any constitution, under an absolute autocrat, and it is their chief pride that their monarch is an irresponsible busybody, whose chief aim is to bother his patient subjects.

This is the "Dutchman" in American eyes; but how does the Yankee look in the imagination of my countrymen? In the German language the adjective "American" is usually connected with but three things. The Germans speak of

American stoves, and mean a kind of stove which I have never seen in this country; they speak of American duels, and mean an absurd sort of duel which was certainly never fought on this continent; and finally, they speak of American humbug, and mean by it that kind of humbug which flourishes in Berlin just as in Chicago. But the American man is of course very well known. He is a haggard creature, with vulgar tastes and brutal manners, who drinks whiskey and chews tobacco, spits, fights, puts his feet on the table, and habitually rushes along in wild haste, absorbed by a greedy desire for the dollars of his neighbors. He does not care for education or art, for the public welfare or for justice, except so far as they mean money to him. Corrupt from top to toe, he buys legislation and courts and government; and when he wants fun, he lynches innocent negroes on Madison Square in New York, or in the Boston Public Garden. He has his family home usually in a sky-scraper of twenty-four stories; his business is founded on misleading advertisements; his newspapers are filled with accounts of murders, and his churches swarm with hypocrites.

It is true that on both sides of the ocean there are some who know a little better; but if the millions who enjoy the New York Journal and the Berliner Lokalanzeiger have such character sketches in mind, how small is the influence on public opinion of that little set which relies on the New York Evening Post and the Nationalzeitung! And even these best classes, are they really so much freer from prejudice? After all, the American clings to the belief that the German is reactionary and subservient, without a manly desire for freedom and independence, — that his Emperor is irresponsible, and the average subject no gentleman; while the American remains to German eyes dollar-thirsty and corrupt, vulgar and selfish, — on the whole, also, no gentleman. So when an English cable agency sends news to Germany that the Americans have fallen upon the poor Cubans to fill the pockets of senators, and are killing in the Philippines mostly women and children, and sends news to America that the Germans are slyly interfering with the navy in Manila or plundering Pekin or preparing a revolution in South America, is it surprising that the worst finds the readiest belief, and that public opinion in both countries cries, "How dare they, the rascals!"

That which alone seems surprising is that the brambles of prejudice can grow so exuberantly while the ocean steamers are crowded, going and coming. The hundreds of students who go yearly to German universities, the thousands of Ameri-

can sight-seers who go every summer on pilgrim-
ages from Heidelberg to Cologne, the millions of
German immigrants who have been poured into
this country, and the billions of newspaper pages
which are printed on both sides every year, — are
they all unable to disseminate the truth? But
we cannot deny that the psychological conditions
are more favorable to the survival of the false
view, in spite of the blessed work of the Associated
Press. The Americans who cross the ocean cannot see much of Germany and cannot teach much
about America. A friend assured me once that
there is only one classification of Americans which
it is worth while to make, — those who have been
abroad and those who have not. I cannot agree
with him. I have met many whose minds have
spanned the world, though they have never left
the New England States, and many more who have
strolled over the whole of Europe, and yet are
as narrow and provincial as if they had never
looked over the fence of their own back yards
A man may heartily enjoy the architecture of
Nürnberg or Hildesheim, the paintings of Dres-
den, the operas of Baireuth, the scenery of the
Black Forest, and the uniforms of the lieutenants
of the guard, and yet leave the country with all
the absurd prejudices which he carried there. We
are inclined by psychological laws to perceive

merely that which we expect to perceive ; we do
not voluntarily suppress the remainder, but it does
not exist for us at all.   Germany has no freedom :
thus the most harmless policeman on the street
corner appears to be a tyrant, and brings before
the mind of the traveler the terrors of mediæval-
ism.   And when the bicycles must have a number by day and a lantern by night, who can help
thinking sentimentally of the free home over the
sea, where everybody has the liberty to run over
his fellow ; and where the landlady gives chops
for breakfast, and not eggs alone ; and where
plenty of blankets, not feather beds, await you ;
and where ice water flows and mince pies abound ?
The little differences trouble the stranger and
they swell in his imagination, while every good
thing that does not fit with his anticipations fades
away and is soon forgotten.   Very few Americans
come into a sufficiently intimate contact with the
real German life to get their traditional errors
eradicated.

But the usual Europe-trotter, on the other hand,
does not help much to propagate the belief in
American culture.   He goes his way quietly, and
no one will blame him for enjoying the view from
Heidelberg Castle down to the Neckar Valley without making a speech for the glory of his country.   He remains unobserved ; but when a puffed-

up parvenu from the West comes along, with noisy manners, he is observed, and he alone, — though one among scores, — is then " the American ; " and if he puts his feet on the table in the hotel corridor, there are certainly a dozen men in the neighborhood who will never after relinquish the opinion that all Americans are hopelessly vulgar and disgusting.

III

The Germans who travel to America either are on a journey or have come to stay. The first group contains few : they go, for the most part, from New York through Florida and the City of Mexico to San Francisco, and through the Yellowstone Park, Chicago, and Quebec back to Hoboken. If they have done that in six months, they write only one or two magazine articles about the Americans; but if they have succeeded in doing it in six weeks, then they write a book, and a big one. They have of course seen everything : they have shaken hands with the President, have witnessed a prize fight at an athletic club, visited the stock yards and the Indian schools, studied polygamy in Utah and the Chinese quarters in San Francisco; they have even met some one in the Pullman car who knew all about the silver question and the next presidency.   And when they have

added their own experiences in the barber shops
and in the barrooms, the book will contain all
that Germans can desire to know about America.
They have not the remotest idea that this nation
can show greater achievements than its hotels and
railways.   They have seen all the Bædeker stars,
and do not guess that the tourist attractions of
this country represent its real energies much less
than do those of Europe.   Europe, with its relics
of history and art, may speak to the eye; America speaks to the understanding; whatever national life is here apparent to the eye is mostly
but an imitation of Europe.   The traveler is
accustomed to open his eyes only, and to close his
ears ; he descants for the thousandth time on the
Rocky Mountains and Niagara, but he does not
learn anything about the inner life, with its
mountains of accomplishment and its cataracts
of problems.   There are plenty of excellent German monographs about special economic features
of American life which can be studied from the
outside ; the studies on the more internal functions of education or religion are much more
superficial, and nothing which really analyzes the
inner man with full understanding has ever been
carried home by the German traveler.   On the
other hand, he is too rare a guest to add anything
by his appearance here to American ideas about

the Germans.   He remains the more unobserved
because there is no lack of German nature already
at hand to be inspected under the most various
conditions; for New York and Chicago have each
more Germans than any German city except Berlin.   Thus only the Germans who live here are
able to represent their native country in the New
World, and to take back to Germany true ideas
about the inner American life.   How has it happened that even these millions have not dispelled
the dense fog of Continental ignorance about the
Yankees?   How has it happened that the real
America is still as undiscovered by the educated
German as if Columbus had never crossed the
ocean?

The German immigrant can justly claim to be
a respectable and very desirable element of the
American population : he has stood always on the
side of solid work and honesty ; he has brought
skill and energy over the ocean, and he has not
forgotten his music and his joyfulness ; he is not
second to any one in his devotion to the duties of
a citizen in peace and in war, and without his aid
many of America's industrial, commercial, and
technical triumphs would be unknown.   But all
that does not disprove the fact that he is often
somewhat unfit to judge fairly the life which surrounds him.   First, he belongs almost always to

a social stratum in which the attention is fully
absorbed by the external life of a country, and
which is without feeling for the achievements of
its mental life; he was poor in his fatherland,
and lives comfortably here, and thus he is enthusiastic over the material life, praises the railroads
and hotels, the bridges and mills, but does not even
try to judge of the libraries and universities, the
museums and the hospitals.   On the other hand,
he feels socially in the background; he is the
" Dutchman," who, through his bad English,
through his habits and manners, through his
tastes and pleasures, is different from the majority, and therefore set apart as a citizen of second
rank, — if not slighted, at least kept in social isolation.   On the side of the German, the result of
this situation is often an entire ignorance of the
Anglo-American life; he may go his way here
for thirty years without ever breaking bread at
the table of any one outside of the German circle;
he may even have become rich, and yet he is not
quite in the social current.   His ignorance is therefore too easily coupled with unfairness; the German who feels himself slighted tends to minimize
the effect of the unfriendly attitude of the Anglo-
American by sharp criticism : everything which
seems strange is in his talk distorted into a defect,
and every real weakness grows to a vice.   Of

course, there are not a few exceptions, not a few
who are fully received, even if we disregard that
less worthy class which buys recognition by dis-
avowal of the fatherland, of whom some, in the
interest of city politics, are said to be ambitious of
becoming Irishmen. The large mass, however,
continues in that social separation which makes its
judgment an odd mixture of ignorance as to the
inner life, unfairness as to the personal qualities,
and blind admiration for the wealth and economic
greatness of this country. In such a form the
gossip of a hundred thousand family letters and
saloon conversations pours into Germany, and
naturally reinforces there, through that which it
praises almost as much as through that which it
blames, the feeling of antipathy toward the United
States. Such German-Americans are not only
unfit to judge Americans; they are also, unfor-
tunately, unfit to correct the traditional ideas of
Americans about Germans. If they lived up to
their highest duty, they would work out in themselves the noblest type of German ideals, in order
to impress Americans with the best of the German
nature, and thus make moral conquests for their
old home. So did the generation of 1848 with a
circle of admirable leaders, of whom Carl Schurz
became the best known representative. But no
new generation has appeared after them to take

up the work, no new set has come in which has
felt itself called upon to add to the glory of the
fatherland. A few high-minded newspapers have
faithfully shown the way; Conried's Irving Place
Theatre has been a source of inspiration with noble
influence on the American stage; a few eminent
scholars are sprinkled over the country. But on
the whole the German-American masses of to-day
show little of the German tendency to higher aims.
They are surprisingly indifferent; their clubs and
associations lack more and more the inspirations
of earlier days, and they are satisfied to praise
honesty as their peculiar German virtue instead of
feeling it to be a matter of course. Alarmingly
few men of individual power have grown up among
those millions. What characterizes the German at
home, the tendency to idealism and the desire for
intellectual life, has evaporated; the artisan or the
farmer, whose highest wish at home would have
been to send his son to the gymnasium, and perhaps even to the university, is here glad if his
boy becomes a clever business clerk as quickly as
possible. It seems too often as if he imitated by
preference the bad features of his surroundings.
The exceptions merely confirm the rule that the
average German-American stands in some respects
below the level of the average German at home.
This is hardly a result of the bad quality of the

immigrants; on the contrary, the factors which determine the individual to cross the ocean make it probable that, in most cases, the stronger and more energetic personalities seek the wider field of a new country; the lowering of the average must be the result of the new conditions of life, and not of the selection of the material.

It seems, then, that the German-Americans have done but little to make the Germans understand America better, and perhaps still less to make the Americans understand the real Germans; they have given little help toward awakening in the two nations the feeling of mutual sympathy; and yet, as we have said, this alone is the way for an organic improvement of their political relations.   If they had lived up to their duties in the last twenty years as they did in the fifties and sixties, the branches of the Teutonic race would have been united by a more cordial feeling, and many occurrences of the last two years would have been impossible.

They alone have seen both countries with loving eyes and loyal hearts, and they ought, therefore, to be able to do justice to the true intentions of both parties.   In their hands is the flag of truce.   They must embody in themselves the best side of the German spirit, and they must open the eyes of Germans at home to what is best in the American nature. Their work must of course be futile if they ignore the facts and tell fairy tales about the two countries. What is needed is nothing but the truth, freed from the traditional phrases of short-sighted prejudice.

To be sure, the atmosphere in which the prejudices take shape would have been different if the Americans of the old stock had shown a deeper understanding or a fairer appreciation of all the desirable features which the German immigration has added to the general American physiognomy. For the last three months of every presidential campaign the German voter is praised up and down as a model citizen and what not. But when the election is over, the Yankee feels himself again as the host who alone has the full right to set standards, and the American " with a hyphen " is the guest who is tolerated, but who has to adjust his ideals to the English ways. He forgets too easily that the American nation is not a nation of Englishmen, but a new English-speaking people, in which the most various elements are fused into something new and original. This new nation, which is so decidedly un-English, not least in its smartness and its humor and its oratorical flow, and which willingly accepts negro songs as its national melodies, ought to welcome gladly the infusion of German blood, instead of

avoiding the social mixture.   It is easy to make
light of the music and the Christmas tree or to
denounce the German breweries, but even the
beer is a gain if it displaces the ruinous whiskey,
and the music and the Christmas tree are merely
symbols of characteristics which were certainly
desirable additions to the temperament of the
new nation.   But there were more important factors, — industry and civic virtues, which, brought
over from Germany, helped to build up the land
and the nation, and it is unfair to stamp the German-American as a citizen of second rank and
thus to isolate him socially.

It is really not surprising that the Germans in
America dislike every approach to England, because they feel instinctively that an Anglo-American union reinforces the feeling that the Americans
are an Anglo-Saxon nation in which other Teutonic elements are strangers.   It was thus only
natural that the rumors of an Anglo-American
alliance a short time ago were the occasion —
the first for many years — of gigantic demonstrations on the part of the Germans in the country.   It was not, as they themselves believed it to
be, a fight against imperialism, as in the question
of imperialism the Germans are just as divided as
any other group of citizens ; and it was still much
less, as the newspapers of Germany believed it to

be, a demonstration against England in favor of
Germany, but it was simply a reaction against the
emphasis of the Anglo-Saxon character of the
American nation, which means a social humil-
iation for the German-Americans. The fault is
thus clearly on both sides; the native Americans
and the German-Americans have participated
equally in bringing about this separation. But
for us it is not a question of blame, merely a
question of fact; and the fact remains, that the
German-American has lived in an isolation which
has made him on the whole unfit for the rôle which
would be most natural to him, that of giving
to the Germans at home and to the Americans
here a deeper mutual understanding of their real
characters.

IV

I may perhaps be allowed to point out, as illustrations, those two prejudices with regard to the
character of the two peoples which strike me as
an impartial observer most strongly, and which are
really the root of the misunderstandings. I mean
the traditional German opinion that the Americans
have no idealism, but are selfish realists, and the
American belief, that the Germans have no spirit
of freedom. The belief that the Americans have
no spark of idealism in their souls has done

more harm to the relations of Continental nations with the United States than any protective tariff or any commercial competition. The largest newspaper of Berlin wrote the other day in a character sketch of the American : " The American does not hesitate to cheat his best friend, but the most astonishing expression of the American lack of conscience is given in politics, which has been transformed by him into a swamp of corruption, detestable as that of Russia and China. Every public office in America is for the office-holder merely an arrangement to steal and to fill his own pockets at the expense of the community. That is the ideal purpose of life for everybody, from the simple alderman up to the senator in Washington. The American is always ready to sacrifice all the interests of the community to his private interests ; the *non olet* of the Emperor Vespasian has changed for him into It smells delightfully ! " For this chance quotation might easily be substituted a hundred others of exactly the same spirit. And such ideas, hammered daily into the mind of the German nation, for whom the honesty and integrity of the civil service is the basis of public life, must necessarily produce an antipathy which makes any understanding difficult. It has surrounded every act of America with a cloud of selfishness and meanness by which even the most harmless action becomes repugnant to sound feelings, and by which the most guileless man is made a prey to the newspapers of Europe. Granted that an American action can never have idealistic motives, it is not difficult to distort daily occurrences and historical events so that everything appears disgusting to a country which believes itself to have a prior claim upon every sort of idealistic feeling, and this emotion of the crowd then becomes the spring of political reactions.

I think this attitude is utterly groundless. More than that, I think the true American is an idealist through and through. I perceive, to be sure, that his idealism is often loose and lax and ineffective, but it remains idealism nevertheless, and he deceives himself when he poses as a realist, like his English cousin. What most quickly misleads is, doubtless, his consuming interest in money-making, together with the sharp struggle for existence, the gigantic scale of his undertakings, his hasty, impulsive movements, his taste for strong sensational stimuli, his spoils politics, and the influence of corporations upon his legislation. But is not all that merely the surface view? The American is not greedy for money; if he were, he would not give away his wealth with such a liberal hand, and would not put aside all the unidealistic

European schemes of money-making which exclude individual initiative, as, for instance, the pursuit of dowries, or, on a lower level, the tipping system. The American runs after money primarily for the pleasure of the chase ; it is the spirit of enterprise that spurs him on, the desire to make use of his energies, to realize his personality. And there is one other factor : in a country where political conditions have excluded titles and orders and social distinctions in general, money is in the end the only means of social discrimination, and financial success becomes thus the measurement of the ability of the individual and of his power to realize himself in action. That the struggle for existence is sharper here than in Europe is simply a fairy tale. In a country where the greatest enterprises are undertaken in the service of charity, and where the natural resources of the land are inexhaustible, even the lowest classes do not struggle for existence, but, seen from the Continental standpoint, merely for comfort; of this the lyrical character of the discussions of social problems here compared with their dramatic character in Germany gives the fullest evidence.

The manners and tastes of individuals are also easily misinterpreted. Those hasty, pushing movements look like an overflow of realistic energies, but they are simply the outcome of a lack of co-

ordination and adjustment. The quiet movements of the Englishman are expressions of
strength and energy ; the hasty movements of the
Yankee and his motor restlessness, manifested in
the use of rocking-chairs and chewing-gum, are
mere imperfections of the motor coördinating
centres, an inability to suppress and to inhibit.
In the same way, the demand for strong stimuli
is not at all a symptom of over-irritation, as those
usually claim it to be who consider American life
a nerve-wearing clash of selfish energies. No, it
is only insufficient training through the lack of
æsthetic traditions. While over-irritation would
demand that the stimuli grow stronger and
stronger, experience shows that they soften and
become more refined from year to year, stamping
to-day as vulgar the acknowledged pleasure of
yesterday. But the most amusing misunderstanding arises when the American himself thinks that
he proves the purely practical character of his
life by the eagerness with which he saves his time,
on the ground that time is money. It strikes me
that, next to the public funds, nothing is so much
wasted here as time. Whether it is wasted in
reading the endless newspaper reports of murder
trials or in sitting on the base-ball grounds, in
watching a variety show or in lying in bed, in
waiting for the elevator or in being shaved after

the American fashion, in attending receptions or in enjoying committee meetings, is quite unessential. The whole scheme of American education is possible only in a country which is rich enough not to need any economy of time, and which can therefore allow itself the luxury of not asking at what age a young man begins to earn his own living. The American shopkeeper opens his store daily one hour later than the German tradesman, and the American physician opens his office three years later than his German colleague of equal education. This may be very good, but it is a prodigality of time which the Germans would be unable to imitate.

Still another prolific source of European comment is the anti-idealistic character of American politics; but the critics overlook certain essential points when they deduce from it the intellectual state of the average citizen. It is, for instance, not at all fair to compare the political German newspapers with those of America, and to consider them as mirrors of the nation. In Germany all the newspapers which have a political value are exclusively for the educated classes, while in America every paper, and especially those which are seen most, is written for the masses. Social economic conditions make that necessary; and it is, therefore, natural that the American paper makes concessions to vulgarity which would be impossible on the other side. Moreover, the critics overlook the fact that the machine politicians are not the representative men of this country. The same complex historical reasons which have made the party spoils system and the boss system practically necessary forms of government have often brought representatives of very vulgar instincts into conspicuous political places; but that does not mean that the higher instincts are absent, still less that the alarming accusations which fill the press have more than a grain of truth in a bushel of denunciation. And, finally, it must be considered that politics in the narrower sense of the word, problems of government and of international relations, which occupy the central place in European public life, have been here, on the whole, in the background as compared with economic questions. These economic questions, the tariff or silver or trusts, naturally appeal to the selfish interests of different groups; and schemes and methods which would be low if applied to controversies genuinely political do not exclude idealism if applied to economic struggles. Wherever such and similar factors are eliminated, the American in politics proves himself the purest idealist, the best men come to the front, the most sentimental motives dominate, and almost no one dares to damage his cause by appealing to selfish instincts. Recent events have once more proved that beyond question. Whatever the senators and sugar men may have thought about it, the people wanted the Cuban war for sentimental reasons; and if the uninformed Continental papers maintain that the desire for war had merely selfish reasons, they falsify history. Is not the whole debate over expansion carried on with highly idealistic arguments on both sides? Did not even the Anglo-American alliance get hold of the nation when the masses found an idealistic halo for it, discovering that those Englishmen whom they wanted to fight two years before were of the same blood and the same traditions as themselves? Is it not entirely sentimental to use Washington's Farewell Address to-day as a living argument with which to determine practical questions? Even the most natural, selfish, and practical instinct can be overcome with the typical American by a catchy sentimental argument.

This high spirit of the individual in politics repeats itself much more plainly in private life, where helpfulness and honesty seem to me the most essential characteristics of the American. Helpfulness shows itself in charity, in hospitality, in projects for education or for public improvements, or in the most trivial services of daily life;

while silent confidence in the honesty of one's fellow men controls practical relations here in a way
which is not known in cautious Europe, and could
not have been developed if that confidence were
not justified.   Add to it the American's grateful-
ness and generosity, his elasticity and his frankness, his cleanliness and his chastity, his humor
and his fairness; consider the vividness of his
religious emotion, his interest in religious and
metaphysical speculation, his eagerness always to
realize the best results of science, — in short, look
around everywhere without prejudice, and you
cannot doubt that behind the terrifying mask of
the selfish realist breathes the idealist, who is controlled by a belief in ethical values.   Unde-
niably, every one of these characteristics may
develop into an absurdity: gratitude may trans-
form the capture of a merchant vessel into a naval
triumph, speculative desire may run into the
blind alleys of spiritualism, fairness may lead to
the defense of the most cranky schemes, and the
wish for steady improvements may chase the reformer from one fad to another ; and yet it is all
at bottom the purest idealism.   Whenever I have
written about America for my German countrymen, I have said: "You are right to hate that
selfish, brutal, vulgar, corrupt American who lives
in your imagination ; but the true American is at

least as much an idealist as yourself, and Emerson comes nearer to representing his spirit than do the editorial writers of the New York Journal." If I had to draw the American with a few lines, I should emphasize three mental elements. All the essential features of his public life spring from the spirit of self-determination, which was developed by his separation from his mother country; the features of his economic life, from the spirit of self-activity which was developed by his pioneer life; and the features of his intellectual life from the spirit of self-perfection, which has a partly utilitarian, partly Puritan origin. Every one of these three strong tendencies involves dangers, but essentially they are forces of purely idealistic power.

V

To-day I am writing for American readers only, and they would not show that fairness which I have just praised if they allowed me to prove the fallacy of prejudices merely when the prejudices exist on the other side, and not when they are themselves at fault. I may, therefore, be permitted to touch at least one of the many preconceived ideas with which the Americans regard the German nation. I choose, as one case among many, the settled opinion that the Germans, the poor suffering subjects of Emperor William, have no liberty; that the men oppress the women, the higher classes oppress the lower classes, the nobility oppresses the people, the army oppresses the civilians, and the Emperor oppresses all together. It must seem to the American newspaper reader as if India and Russia and Turkey had combined to invent the machinery of German civilization, in which the soldiers are tortured, the laborers imprisoned, the radicals treated as criminals, the women treated as slaves or as dolls, and the king treated as infallible. To be sure, such a text is not unknown in Germany itself; the orators of the Social Democratic party would heartily applaud it, but it would not be the most effective party cry of the demagogues if the spirit of freedom were not the deepest element of the German nature, and the warning that their freedom is threatened the most exciting stimulus. Those, however, who do not wish for a distortion of the facts are sure that there is no people under the sun with more valuable inner freedom than the Germans, who, since Luther and Kant, have started every great movement toward freedom, and who would not have been at the head of the world of science for centuries had not freedom of thought been their life element, and the German university the freest place on earth.

Moreover, if I consider the outer forms of life, I do not hesitate to maintain that Germany is even in that respect freer than the United States. The right to insult the President, and to cross the railroad tracks where it is dangerous, and to ignore the law if a great trust stands behind one, and to spread the poison of anarchistic doctrines, is not freedom, but lack of social development, the survival of a lower civilization, a pseudo-freedom whose symptoms, fortunately, are disappearing from year to year in this country also. And they will disappear still more rapidly now, since the echo of the shot in Buffalo will not die out soon. The people will understand that not only the Polish and Italian fanatics who shoot and stab are guilty, but those who allow anarchy to be preached. However, the suppression of such doctrines of lawlessness is impossible if the principle is not acknowledged that the state has the right and the duty to limit speech for the protection of its possessions, — and no possession is greater than the authority belonging to our highest office, which is impugned not by the anarchist only, but by every one who uses vile language against the President. Freedom is not absence of limitations. The social intercourse of the well-mannered is not less free than that of ill-bred men, though they obey many more rules, and the expression of thought is not less free when we obey the laws of good language; no, it is freer than the expression of those who speak slang. Germans live under more complicated and systematized rules than Americans, and for this very reason they have greater freedom than is possible in the less restrained rush of American life.

The most typical case is, of course, that of the political government. The American takes it for granted that the republican state form represents a higher level than the monarchical one, and that therefore the German who comes to these shores must feel as if he were coming out into the fresh air from a prison. The educated Germans at home feel that it is with the monarchy as with the church. Too many men are adherents of the church from low motives, from fear and superstition and laziness. When such narrow-minded persons become freethinkers and reject the church, they manifest individual progress; but that does not mean that destructive skepticism represents the highest possible relation to the church, and that to become an adherent of the church means falling back to the lower stage. On the contrary, the step from skeptical enlightenment to an ethical belief is in every respect progress: it is the step from rationalism to idealism. The church can thus stand for the lowest and for the highest,

and those who are in the middle, and have not
yet reached the last stage, may well think that the
highest is below their level. Just this manifoldness of stages, the Germans maintain, characterizes the forms of states. To be sure, the mob is
monarchical from low motives, and those who hold
that the business of the state must be in the hands
of a man whom the majority has selected certainly
represent a higher moral stratum than those who
support the throne from selfishness and laziness
and cowardice. But again, a higher standpoint is
possible. The true belief in monarchy means the
belief in symbols which characterizes historical
thinking as over against naturalistic thinking.
And a monarch, as the historical symbol of the
emotional ideals of a nation, wholly outside of the
field of political struggles and elections, needs that
symbolic protection against reproach which appears, seen from a purely materialistic point of
view, as the ridiculous punishment of *lèse-majesté*.
The same is true of all the symbolic values which
radiate from the centre : the titles and degrees and
decorations representing social differentiation seem
childish to an eye which sees the world merely as
a naturalistic mechanism, but invaluable to the
eye which traces the outlines of the historical
spirit in the world. Without differentiation there
can be no complicated social life; until the stage

of symbolic thinking is reached, quantitative differences must furnish the tags, and money furnish
the only standard. But the flag is more than
a piece of cloth, and the higher development of
symbols means a higher civilization. The American who, from the standpoint of his naturalistic
thinking, looks down contemptuously on the German social and political organization hinders, so
it seems to the foreigner, the progress of his own
country; America has become too great to stop
at a social philosophy characteristic of the eighteenth century. An heroic revival is at hand, imperialism awakens echoes throughout the land,
and days are near when Americans will understand better what we mean by the symbols of
German history, and that it is not lack of freedom that prevents us from believing overmuch in
majority votes and the dogma of equality.

But I am not at all afraid to turn the discussion from the philosophical to the practical side,
from the idea of monarchy to the present Emperor. I think there is no other man with whom
the American newspapers have been sc successful
in substituting the caricature for the real portrait.
The irony of the case lies in the fact that the hundreds of amusing stories about the Emperor all
come from the camp of those bureaucrats with
whom the Americans would sympathize least of

all. There is nothing more incompatible with the
American spirit than the temper of the pedants
whose petty purposes the papers here have furthered, while there is nothing more in accord
with the American mood than the true nature of
the Kaiser. The one living American whose personality most closely resembles that of the Emperor William is the brilliant young President of
the United States, who would have been elected
as leader of the nation a few years hence if fate
had saved his beloved predecessor. The Germans
feel in the same way ; if Germany were to become a republic, the people would shudder at
the thought of having one of the parliamentary
leaders of to-day or an average general become
President, but they would elect the present Emperor with enthusiasm as the first President; he
is the most interesting, energetic, talented, industrious, and conscientious personality of our
public life. Those, however, who maintain that
the Emperor is an autocrat do not understand how
closely the German monarchy, not only through
the constitutional and parliamentary limitations
imposed upon it, but still more in its inner forces,
is identical with the national will. The powers
of the American President, far greater than those
of the English King, are especially with respect
to foreign politics not at all less than those of the

German ruler. A President whose ministers cannot be interpellated by the parliament, and whose word can practically turn peace into war and alliance into annexation, in short, with tremendous powers, parties in the grasp of bosses, city administrations under the whip of spoilsmen, the economic world under the tyranny of trusts, and all together under the autocracy of yellow-press editors — No, I love and admire America, but Germany really seems to me freer.

I have tried to show that it is equally one-sided and unfair for the Germans to maintain that the Americans have no idealism, and for the Americans to maintain that the Germans have no sense of freedom; the two cases served merely as chance illustrations, instead of which I could have chosen many others. Wherever we look we find the same fact; that the two great nations see each other through distorting spectacles, and do not understand each other's real character. They misinterpret mere gestures, and therefore do not see the deeper similarity of their natures and their ideals. All this, of course, does not suggest that they are without important differences, but the differences seem to me much more the results of outer conditions than of character. In the outer conditions no stronger contrast is possible, — the Americans with a new national culture in an un-

developed realm of immense material resources ;
the Germans in a realm of limited resources,
but with an old traditional culture.   An old traditional culture signifies a system of institutions
in which the best spirit of past efforts is condensed, and into which the individual is put by
birth. The individual may be low-minded, and
yet he must move in the given tracks, and is thus
shaped to ends nobler than his own.   The result
is that, in Germany, the institutions are often better than the individuals, the forms of civilization
higher than their wearers, the public conscience
wider awake than the private.   In the United
States, with its new culture, just the opposite condition must prevail; the individuals are better,
much better, than the institutions ; the individuals are thoroughly idealistic, while the external
forms of social life are by no means penetrated to
the same degree with the idealistic spirit; they
are still too often the survivals of the time when
the new land had to be opened in a severe struggle
for livelihood, and the commercial resources had
to be developed at all costs.   Consequently, these
forms are now on as great a scale as the resources
themselves, but they appeal still too often to the
lower instincts, and too often tend to pull men
down instead of raising them up.   The individual
conscience is here higher than the public con-

science; individual initiative and responsibility are wonderful, but the encouragement and inspiration which come to the individual from his public institutions are inadequate.

The psychical effect of this situation is a necessary one. In Germany, where the institutions take the lead, the result is that the average man too easily believes he has fulfilled his duty when he appears to satisfy the public requirements, and the spirit of individual initiative therefore slumbers. In America this danger certainly does not exist, but the dangers resulting from the lack of inspiring energy in the centre are not less. Instead of reinforcing the highest emotions, the institutions adjust themselves to the lower instincts, and the psychological effect is that the higher energies are repressed, and the feeling of duty becomes less urgent in public life. We see the newspapers crowded with matter adapted to the lowest tastes of the mob, political results determined by appeals to the most selfish desires, the theatres relying upon the cheapest vaudeville, the churches filled and sermons made attractive by sensational and trivial matters, — everywhere the same willingness to do what the public likes, and nowhere the question what the public ought to have. And this spirit must slowly undermine every public function. Such a system inevitably provides a hothouse of mediocrity; where there exists no social premium upon the highest efforts toward ideal interests, where no general appreciation stimulates individual energies, there is no maximum effect to be expected. The good personal material secures a high average, but no great men; everywhere fair solid work, nowhere a masterpiece; ten thousand excellent public lectures every winter, and not one great thought. The social psychologist who begins to analyze the respective national characters has thus no reason for mere eulogy; he sees shortcomings and defects on both sides, and sees still more clearly how much the two nations might learn from each other. But he does not find traces of those characteristics which in each arouse the disrespect and disgust of the other. The Germans are not servile and reactionary, the Americans are not corrupt and materialistic and brutal. The two peoples are different, but the differences are of a kind, which suggests mutual supplementation and interest in each other, not antipathy and aversion. Neither one is made up of angels, but of men who would like each other most sincerely if their foolish narrow-minded prejudices were removed. These prejudices alone in regard to character, and no objective reason, have brought about the mood that occasions petty quarrels and unnecessary friction between Germans and Americans, that is, between the two most healthy, most vigorous, most promising, and at the same time most similar nations of all which have entered on the twentieth century.

II

EDUCATION

I

I FEEL myself on the whole pretty free from autobiographical tendencies; I am quite ready to double the number of my years, at least, before I begin on memories and confessions. At one point only has the desire for an autobiographical eruption grown in me steadily: I am impelled to tell the story of my school time.

I remember exactly how the impulse took shape in my mind. It was at a teachers' meeting. The teachers were discussing how to relieve the over-burdening of the school children, and how to make tolerable the drudgery of the classroom. Some demonstrated that all the trouble came from the old-fashioned idea of prescribed courses: if the courses were freely chosen, according to the talents and interests of the pupils, their sufferings would be ended. Others maintained that the teachers were guilty: that they did not know enough about educational aims, about child study and psychology and the theory of education. What else than drudgery was to be expected,

under such inadequate pedagogues ? The fight
between the two parties went on with an inspiring
fullness of argument, and thus I fell into a deep
and sound sleep.   And the sleep carried me away
from the elms of New England to my dear old
home on the shore of the Baltic Sea, where I spent
my school days.   I saw once more my classmates
and my teachers ; I strolled once more, as a little
boy with my schoolbooks, through the quaint
streets of Danzig ; I passed again through the
feelings of more than twenty years ago.   Suddenly I awoke at the stroke of the gavel of the
chairman, who solemnly announced that the majority had voted for a compromise : the community ought to see to it that both free election
and the pedagogical information of the teachers
were furthered.   At this point the meeting was
adjourned, and the teachers went to the next hall
for luncheon : there some minor speeches were
served up, on the pernicious influence of the classical languages, and on the value of stenography
and typewriting for a liberal education.   It was
then that the autobiography budded in my mind.
My instinct told me that I must make haste in
the undertaking ; for if I should hear for some
years to come all these sighs of pity for those who
were instructed without election and pedagogy, I
might finally get confused, and extend the same

pity to my own childhood, convinced that my
school life was a deplorable misfortune. I hasten,
therefore, to publish this chapter of my life's
story as advance sheets, some decades before the
remainder, at a period when the gap of time is
still small enough to be bridged by a fair memory.

My great-grandfather lived in Silesia. But
perhaps it may be too long a story if I develop
my case from its historical beginning ; I will
shorten it by saying at once that I entered the
gymnasium in Danzig at nine years of age, and
left it at eighteen. I had previously attended
a private preparatory school, and subsequently I
went to the universities of Leipzig and Heidelberg. It is the gymnasium period of which I wish
to speak. I have no right to boast of it ; I was
a model neither of industry nor of carefulness. I
was not quite so bad as some of my best friends
among my classmates, but I see, with real repent-
ance, from the reports which I have carefully
kept together, that I was not attentive enough in
Latin grammar ; it seems that in the lower classes,
also, my French did not find the full appreciation
of my teachers, and I should feel utterly ashamed
to report what their misled judgment recorded of
my singing and drawing. I was just a fair average. The stages of knowledge which we reached
may most easily be characterized by a comparison

with the standards of New England. At fifteen years I was in *Untersekunda;* and there is not the slightest doubt that, at that stage, all my classmates were prepared to pass the entrance examinations for Harvard College. As a matter of course, German must here be substituted for English, German history and literature for the English correspondents. We should have chosen, at our entrance, that scheme in which both Latin and Greek are taken. The *Abiturientenexamen* at the end of the school time, the examination which opens the door to the university, came three years later. It was a difficult affair, somewhat more difficult than in recent years; and, from a pretty careful analysis of the case, I can say that very few Harvard students have entered the senior class who would have been able to pass that examination respectably. In the smaller colleges of the country, the senior might be expected to reach that level at graduation. No doubt, even after substituting German for English, almost every senior may have taken one or many courses which lie fully outside of the circle in which we moved. The college man who specializes in political economy or philosophy or chemistry from his freshman year knows, in his special field, far more than any one of us knew; but if we take a composite picture of all seniors, the boy who leaves the gym-

nasium is not at a disadvantage in the comparison
of intellectual physiognomy, although far less mature, conformant to his much lower age. If any
man in Dartmouth or Amherst takes his bachelor's degree with that knowledge in mathematics,
history, geography, literature, Latin, Greek,
French, and physics which we had on leaving
school, he is sure to graduate with honors. Our
entrance into the university can thus be compared
merely with the entrance into the post-graduate
courses. Our three highest gymnasium classes
alone correspond to the college; and whoever
compares the German university with the American college, instead of with the graduate school, is
misled either by the age of the students or by the
external forms of student life and instruction.

I reached thus, at the end of my school time,
as a pupil of average standing, the scholarly level
of an average college graduate in this country.
I was then eighteen years of age; the average
bachelor of arts is at least three years older. How
did that difference come about? The natural explanation of the case is that we poor boys were
overburdened, systematically tortured by a cruel
system of overwork, which absorbed all our energies for the one goal, the passing of the examination. I do not dare to contradict this. But the one
thing I may claim in favor of this scheme of over-

loading is the wonderful skill with which the school administration was able to hide these evident facts so completely from our eyes that neither my classmates nor I, nor our parents, nor our teachers themselves, ever perceived the slightest trace of them. The facts were so shamelessly concealed from us that we poor deceived boys thought all the time that the work was a pleasure, that we had leisure for everything, and that we were all as happy as the day was long.

I think that I spent, during all those ten years, about three hours a day in the fresh air, walking and playing, swimming and skating; yet I found time from my ninth year to practice on the violoncello one hour every day, and the novels which I wrote may have lacked everything else, but they never lacked length. Besides such individual schemes to fill our vacant time, we coöperated for that purpose in clubs, from the lowest classes to the highest: at ten years we played instructive games; at twelve years we read classical dramas, each taking one rôle; at fifteen we read papers on art and literature; and at seventeen we had a regular debating club. And all the time, at every stage, there were private theatricals, and excursions into the country, and dancing lessons, and horseback-riding, and coeducation with the education left out; for the poor overburdened girls helped us to bear the load by suffering in common.

Every one of us had, of course, the minor special interests and amusements which suited his own taste ; there was no lack of opportunity to follow up these inclinations ; to use the terminology of modern pedagogy, we " found " ourselves. I found myself, too ; but — and in this respect I did not behave exactly according to the prescribed scheme of this same pedagogy, I am sorry to say — I found myself every two or three years, as some one very different from the former individual whom I had had the pleasure to discover. In the first years of my school time botany was all my desire. We lived in the summer in a country house with a large garden, and a forest near the garden ; and every minute I could spare belonged to the plants which I collected and pressed. It became a boyish passion. If I had to write a novel, this feature of the botanical enthusiasm of the boy would be a very poor invention, if the final outcome were to be a being who has hardly the talent to discriminate a mushroom from an apple tree, and for whom nothing in the world appears so dry as squeezed plants. But I have not to invent here : I am reporting. I thus confess frankly my weakness for dissected vegetables : it lasted about three years. Then came my passion for physical instruments: an uncle gave me on my birthday some dainty little electrical machines, and soon the whole house was overspun with electrical wires. I was thus, at twelve years, on the best road to discover the patent-hunter in my personality, when a friend with theological inclinations interfered: we began to study comparative religion, Islamism in particular. Thus, at fifteen years of age, we learned Arabic from the grammar, and read the Koran. Now, finally, my true nature was found; my friend wrote prophetically in my album that we should both go out as missionaries to the Arabs, — and yet I missed the connection, and went to Boston instead of to Mecca, and forgot on the way all my Arabic. But trouble began soon afterward, — friends of mine found, in digging on their farm, an old Slavic grave containing interesting urns. I became fascinated by ethnological discoveries, and, as important excavations were going on in the neighborhood of my native town, I spent every free afternoon and whole vacation weeks in the ethnological camp, studied the literature of the subject, and dug up urns for our town museum, and wrote, at the age of seventeen, a never published book on the prehistoric anthropology of West Prussia. Then the happy school days came to an end, and yet I had not found myself. I

have never digged any more. I did not become
an ethnologist, and if a visitor to Cambridge
insists on my showing him the Harvard sights,
and we come into the ethnological museum, the
urns bore me so utterly that it is hard for me to
believe that in earlier days they made all my
happiness. I went, then, to the university with
something like a liberal education; supplemented
the school studies by some broader studies in literature, science, and philosophy; and when, in
the middle of my philosophical studies, I came to
psychology, the lightning struck. Exactly ten
years after leaving school, years devoted to psychological studies and psychological teaching in
German universities, Harvard called me over the
ocean as professor of psychology. I thus found
my life work; and in all these years I have never
had an hour in which I doubted that it was my
life work. Yet I did not approach it, in spite of
all those various fanciful interests, before I reached
the intellectual level of the graduate school.

II

I have spoken of these boyish passions not only
to show that we had an abundance of free time
and the best opportunities for the growth of
individual likings, but for the purpose of empha-
sizing — and I add this with all the gratitude of

my heart to my parents, my teachers, and the community — that the school never took the smallest account of those inclinations, and never allowed me to take the slightest step aside from the prescribed school work. My school work was not adjusted to botany at nine years because I played with an herbarium, and at twelve to physics because I indulged in noises with home-made electric bells, and at fifteen to Arabic, an elective which I miss still in several high schools, even in Brookline and Roxbury. The more my friends and I wandered afield with our little superficial interests and talents and passions, the more was the straightforward earnestness of the school our blessing; and all that beautified and enriched our youth, and gave to it freshness and liveliness, would have turned out to be our ruin, if our elders had taken it seriously, and had formed a life's programme out of petty caprices and boyish inclinations. I still remember how my father spoke to me, when I was a boy of twelve. I was insisting that Latin would be of no use to me, as I should become a poet or a physicist. He answered : " If a lively boy has to follow a country road, it is a natural and good thing for him to stroll a hundred times from the way, and pick flowers and run for butterflies over the fields on both sides of the road. But if we say to him, 'You need not keep the road; follow your butterflies,' where will he find himself at nightfall?"

My question was, how our German school made it possible to bring us so much more quickly, without overburdening us, to the level of the American senior. I have given so far only a negative characteristic of the school in saying that it made no concession to individual likings and preferences: that is, of course, not a sufficient explanation. If I think back, I feel sure that the chief source of this success was the teachers. But in regard to the teachers, also, I may begin with a negative statement: our teachers did not know too much about the theory of education, or about the history of pedagogy or psychology; and while I heard about some of them gossip of a rather malicious kind, I never heard that any one of them had read a book on child study. The other day I found in a paper on secondary education a lamentation to this effect: that the American schools have still many teachers who have no reflective theories on the aim with which they teach their subjects, and the educational values which belong to them. The author said: "I shall not soon forget the surprise with which an intelligent teacher said to me, not long ago, 'An aim! I have no aim in teaching; that is a new idea.'" "Such teachers of Latin and algebra," the author compassionately added, "meant that the choice of these subjects as fit subject-matter of instruction was no concern of theirs; they taught these subjects as best they could, because these subjects were in the course of study." Exactly such old-fashioned teachers were ours. My literature teacher was never troubled by the suspicion that literature may be less useful than meteorology and organic chemistry, neither of which had a place in our school; and if some one had asked my Greek teacher, "What is the value of the instruction in Greek? What is your aim in reading Sophocles and Plato with your young friends in the class?" he would have answered that he had never thought about it, any more than why he was willing to breathe and to live. He taught his Greek as best he could in the place to which he was called, but he certainly never took it as his concern to reflect whether Greek instruction ought not, after all, to be discontinued; he left that to the principal and to the government. His Plato and his Sophocles, his Homer and his Thucydides, were to him life and happiness, and to share them with us was an instinctive desire, which would have lost its enthusiasm and inspiration if he had tried to base it on arguments.

But this thought has led me from the negative

characteristics of my teachers to a positive one, —
yes, to the most positive one which I felt in them,
— to the one which was the real secret of our German school : my teachers were enthusiastic on the
subjects they taught, as only those who know
them thoroughly ever can be.   I had no teacher
who hastily learned one day what he must teach
me the next; who was satisfied with second-hand
knowledge, which is quite pretty for entertain-
ment and orientation, but which is so intolerable
and inane when we come to distribute it and to
give it to others.   I had from my ninth year no
teacher in any subject who had not completed
three years' work in the graduate school.   Even
the first elements of Greek and mathematics, of
history and geography, were given to us by men
who had reached the level of the doctorate, and
who had the perspective of their own fields.
They had seen their work with the eye of the
scholar, and thus even the most elementary material of their science was raised to the height of
scholarly interest.   Elements taken for themselves
alone are trivial and empty everywhere, and to
teach them is an intolerable drudgery, which fills
the schoolroom with dullness and the pupils with
aversion.   Elements as the introductory part of
a scholarly system are of ever new and fascinating interest, more promising and enjoyable

than any complex problems. A great poet once said that any man who has ever really loved in his youth can never become quite unhappy in life. A man who has ever really taken a scholarly view of his science can never find in that science anything which is quite uninteresting. Such enthusiasm is contagious. We boys felt that our teachers believed with the fullness of their hearts in the inner value of the subjects, and every new bit of knowledge was thus for us a new revelation. We did not ask whether it would bake bread for us. We were eager for it on account of its own inner richness and value; and this happy living in an atmosphere of such ideal belief in the inner worth and glory of literature and history, of science and thought, was our liberal education.

I know it would be wrong to explain our being three years ahead of a New England boy merely from the scholarly preparation of our teachers. A second factor, which is hardly less important, stands clear before my mind, too, — the help which the school found in our homes. I do not mean that we were helped in our work, but the teachers were silently helped by the spirit which prevailed in our homes with regard to the school work. The school had the right of way; our parents reinforced our belief in the work and our respect

for the teachers. A reprimand in the school was
a shadow on our home life ; a word of praise in
the school was a ray of sunshine for the household. The excellent schoolbooks, the wise plans
for the upbuilding of the ten years' course, the
hygienic care, the external stimulations, — all, of
course, helped toward the results ; and yet I am
convinced that their effect was entirely secondary
compared with these two features, — the scholarly
enthusiasm of our teachers and respect for the
school on the part of our parents.

No man can jump over his shadow. I cannot suddenly leave all my memories and experiences behind me, and when I behold the onward
rush of our school reformers, I cannot forget
my past ; I may admire their good will, but I
cannot accept their bad arguments. I do not
speak here as a psychologist ; I know quite well
that some consider the psychologist a pedagogical
expert, who brings the profoundest information
directly from his laboratory to the educational
witness stand. No such power has come to me.
I do not know whether my professional brethren
have had pleasanter experiences, but I have
always found psychology silent as a sphinx, when
I came to her with the question of what we ought
to do in the walks of practical life. When I
asked her about the true and the false, she was

most loquacious; but when I came to her about
the good and the bad, seeking advice and help,
she never vouchsafed me a word. I confess that
I have, therefore, slowly become a little skeptical
as to whether she is really more communicative
with my psychological friends, or whether they do
not simply take her perfect silence for a welcome
affirmation of all their own thoughts and wishes.
I thus come to the question of school reform without any professional authority; I come to it simply with the warm interest of a man who has
children in the schools, who has daily contact with
students just out of school, and who has not forgotten his own school time.

III

The most essential feature of all recent school
reforms — or, with a less question-begging title,
I should say school experiments — has been the
tendency toward elective studies. But I am in
doubt whether we should consider it really as one
tendency only; the name covers two very different
tendencies, whose practical results are externally
similar. We have on one side the desire to adjust
the school work to the final purposes of the individual in practical life; which means beginning
professional preparation in that period which up
to this time has been given over to liberal educa-

tion. We have on the other side the desire to adjust the school work to the innate talents and likings of the individual, which means giving in the school work no place to that which finds inner resistance in the pupil. In the first case the university method filters down to the school; in the second case the kindergarten method creeps up to the school. In the one case the liberal education of the school is replaced by professional education; in the other case the liberal education is replaced by liberal play. If one of the two tendencies were working alone, its imminent danger would be felt at once; but as they seem to coöperate, the one working from the bottom and the other from the top, each hides for the moment the defects of the other. And yet the coincidence is almost accidental and entirely superficial; both desire to make concessions to individual differences. Peter and Paul ought not to have the same school education we are told; but the essential question of what, after all, Peter ought to learn in school must be answered very differently, according as we look at it from the point of view of the kindergarten or from the point of view of professional life; as there is indeed a difference whether I ask what may best suit the taste and liking of Peter, the darling, or whether I ask what Peter, the man, will need for the battle of life, in which nobody asks what he likes, but where the question is how he is liked, and how he suits the tastes of his neighbors. The one method treats the boy as a child, and the other treats the boy as a man. Nothing is common to them, after all, except the result that boyhood loses its opportunity for a liberal education, which ought to borrow from the kindergarten merely its remoteness from practical professional life, and from professional work merely its seriousness.

Neither tendency stands alone in our social life. In short, the one fits the mercenary spirit of our time, and the other fits its spirit of selfish enjoyment. From the standpoint of social philosophy, mercenary utilitarianism and selfish materialism belong together; everywhere do they grow together, and everywhere do they fight together against the spirit of idealism. But while they fight together, they march to the battlefield on very different roads. Practical life demands division of labor, and, therefore, the specialization of the individual. The argument which urges the earliest possible beginning of this specialization is thus a natural one, and the conviction that the struggle for existence must become more difficult with the growing complexity of modern life may encourage the view that the

remedy lies in professional training at the expense
of all other education.   The lawyer and the physician need so many facts for the efficiency of
their work that it seems a waste of energy to burden the future lawyer with the knowledge of natural sciences, and the future physician with the
knowledge of history.   If this is true, however,
we ought to begin still earlier : on the first day in
the kindergarten, I should show my little lawyer
two cakes, and explain to him that one is his cake,
and the other is not, — social information which
does not lie in the line of my little naturalist;
and I should tell the other little fellow that one
cake has plums and the other has not, — scientific
instruction which is without value for the future
lawyer.   But even if I shape my school according
to such schemes, do I really reach, after all, the
goal at which I am aiming?   Does not the utilitarian spirit deceive itself ?   And even if we do
not acknowledge any other standpoint than the
mercenary one, is not the calculation very superficial ?   The laborer in the mill may be put, sometimes, by the cruelty of the age of steam, in a
place where his personality as a whole is crippled,
and only one small function is in use; but the
higher the profession, the more nearly is the
whole man working in every act, and the more,
therefore, is a broad general education necessary

to practical efficiency. The biologists tell us that the play of animals is a biologically necessary preparation for the struggle of existence, and that in a parallel way, the playing of the child is the wise scheme of nature to prepare man in some respect for the struggles of life. How infinitely more necessary for the battles of manhood, though seemingly of no more practical use than such play, is the well-planned liberal education!

The higher the level on which the professional specializing begins, the more effective it is. I have said that we German boys did not think of any specialization and individual variation before we reached a level corresponding to the college graduation here. In this country, the college must still go on for a while playing the double rôle of the place for the general education of the one, and the workshop for the professional training of the other; but at least the high school ought to be faithful to its only goal of general education without professional anticipations. Moreover, we are not only professional wage-earners; we live for our friends and our nation; we face social and political, moral and religious problems; we are in contact with nature and science, with art and literature; we shape our town and our time; and the experience is common to every one, to the banker and the manufacturer, to the minister and the teacher, to the lawyer and the physician. The technique of our profession, then, appears only as a small variation of the large background of work in which we all share; and if the education must be adapted to our later life, all these problems demand a uniform education for the members of the same social community. The division of labor lies on the outside. We are specialists in our handiwork, but our heart work is uniform, and the demand for individualized education emphasizes the small differences in our tasks, and ignores the great similarities.

And after all, who is able to say what a boy of twelve years will need for his special life work? It is easily said in a school programme that the course will be adapted to the needs of the particular pupil with respect to his later life, but it would be harder to say how we are to find out what the boy does need; and even if we know it, the straight line to the goal is not always the shortest way.

The one need of my individual fate, compared with that of other German boys, is the English language, and the one great blank in the prescribed programme of our gymnasium was the total absence of instruction in English. Yet I have such unlimited confidence in the wisdom of my teachers that I cannot help thinking they knew

quite well how my case stood. I can imagine that
when I was twelve years old, the principal of the
school said in a faculty meeting : " This boy will
need the English language later, to philosophize
on the other side of the ocean, and he ought to
begin now to learn it, in time for his professional
work ; to get the free time for it we must eliminate the Greek from his course." But then my
dear little gray-haired Greek teacher must have
arisen and have said with indignation : " No, sir :
the bit of English which is necessary to lecture to
students, and to address teachers' meetings, and
to write for the Atlantic Monthly can be learned
at any time, but Greek he will never learn if he
does not learn it now ; and if he does not have it,
he will never get that inspiration which may make
his scholarly work worth calling him over the
ocean. Only if he studies Greek will they call
him to use English ; but if he learns only English, he never will have the chance to use it."
That settled my case, and so came about the curious chance that I accepted the professorship at
Harvard without having spoken a single word of
English in my life ; and I still thank my old
Greek teacher, who is long since dead, for his
decision. Yes, as I think it over, I am inclined
to believe that it is just so in most cases : if we
prepare for the one thing, we shall have a chance

for the other; but if we wisely prepare at once for the other, our chance for it will never come. Life is, after all, not so easily manufactured as the advertising circular of a private boarding school, in which everything is exactly adapted to the individual needs.

This elective adjustment of the studies to the later professional work and business of the man plays a large part in the theoretical discussions, and there acts effectively on the crowd through the promise of professional success; but it strikes me that this utilitarian appeal works, on the whole, for the interest of that other kind of electivism which promises ease through the adjustment of the school to the personal inclinations. It seems to me that, in the practical walks of education, this is by far the stronger impulse to election. Even in the college, where most boys have at least a dim idea of what they want to do in life, the election with reference to the later occupation usually plays a secondary rôle; liking is the great ruler. The university method were powerless in the school reform, did it not act as agent for the kindergarten method. This leading plea for electives takes the following form : All instruction must be interesting ; if the pupil's interest is not in it, the whole instruction is dead matter, useless vexation. Everything which appeals to the natural tastes and instincts of the child is interesting. Instruction, therefore, must be adjusted to the natural instincts and tastes.

The logical fallacy of this ought to be evident. All instruction which is good must be interesting; but does it follow therefrom that all instruction which is interesting must also be good? Is it not possible that there are kinds of interest which are utterly bad and destructive? All that appeals to the natural tastes and instincts is interesting; does it follow that nothing is interesting which goes beyond the natural instincts? Is it not savage life to follow merely the instincts and natural desires? Is not all the meaning of education just to discriminate between good and bad desires? to suppress the lower instincts, and to reinforce the higher; above all, to awake new desires, to build up new interests, to create new instincts? If civilization, with its instruments of home and school education, could not overcome our natural tastes and instinctive desires, we should remain forever children whose attention is captured by everything that excites and shines. The street tune would expel the symphony, the prize fight would overcome the drama, the yellow press and the dime novel would be our literature; our social life would be vulgar, our public life hysterical, and our intellectual life a mixture of cheap gossip and sensational news with practical schemes for comfort and advertisement. Yes, instruction must be full of interest; but whether instruction is good or bad, is in the spirit of civilization or against it, depends upon the question what sort of interest is in the play, — that which vulgarizes, or that which refines; that which the street boy brings from the slums to the school, or that which the teacher brings from the graduate school to the country classroom. The more internal the motives which capture the attention, the higher the mental functions to which we appeal, the more we are really educators. The platform is no variety show; the boys must be inspired, but not amused.

I am not afraid to push my heresy even to the point of seeing with serious doubts the rapidly growing tendency toward the demonstrative method in scientific instruction. No doubt all such illustrations strongly appeal to common sense; our happy children, the public thinks, see and touch everything, where we had only words on words. But the words appealed to a higher power than the demonstrations, — those spoke to the understanding, these to the perception; those gave us the laws, these the accidental realizations. No demonstration, no experiment, can really show us the totality of a law; it shows us

always only one special case, which as such is
quite unimportant. Its importance lies in the
necessity which can be expressed merely by words,
and never by apparatus. The deeper meaning of
naturalistic instruction is by far more fully present in the book than in the instrument; and
while it is easier to teach and to learn natural
science when it appeals to the eye rather than to
the reason, I doubt whether it has, from a higher
standpoint, the same educational value, just as I
doubt whether the doll with a silk dress and a
phonograph in the chest has the same value for
the development of the child at play that the simple little wooden doll has. The question of scientific instruction is, of course, far too complex to
be analyzed here; the method of demonstrations
has some good features; and above all, the other
kind of instruction, to be valuable at all, needs
much better teachers than those whom the schools
have at their disposal. I wish only to point out
that even here, where the popular agreement is
unanimous, very serious hesitation is possible.

I have spoken of the damage to the subject-
matter of instruction, which results from the limitation of the work to personal taste; but there
is also a formal side of education, which is to me
more important. A child who has himself the
right of choice, or who sees that parents and

teachers select the courses according to his tastes
and inclinations, may learn a thousand pretty
things, but never the one which is the greatest of
all : to do his duty.   He who is allowed always to
follow the paths of least resistance never develops
the power to overcome resistance ; he remains utterly unprepared for life.   To do what we like to
do, — that needs no pedagogical encouragement :
water always runs downhill.   Our whole public
and social life shows the working of this impulse,
and our institutions outbid one another in cater-
ing to the taste of the public.   The school alone
has the power to develop the opposite tendency,
to encourage and train the belief in duties and
obligations, to inspire devotion to better things
than those to which we are drawn by our lower
instincts.   Yes, water runs downhill all the time ;
and yet all the earth were sterile and dead if water
could not ascend again to the clouds, and supply
rain to the field which brings us the harvest. We
see only the streams going down to the ocean ; we
do not see how the ocean sends up the waters to
bless our fields.   Just so do we see in the streams
of life the human emotions following the impulses
down to selfishness and pleasure and enjoyment,
but we do not see how the human emotions ascend
again to the ideals, — ascend in feelings of duty and
enthusiasm ; and yet without this upward move-

ment our fields were dry, our harvest lost. That
invisible work is the sacred mission of the school;
it is the school that must raise man's mind from
his likings to his belief in duties, from his instincts
to his ideals, that art and science, national honor
and morality, friendship and religion, may spring
from the ground and blossom.

IV

But I go further : are elective studies really
elected at all ? I mean, do they really represent
the deeper desires and demands of the individual,
or do they not simply express the cumulation of a
hundred chance influences ? I have intentionally
lingered on the story of my shifting interests in
my boyhood; it is more or less the story of every
halfway-intelligent boy or girl. A little bit of
talent, a petty caprice favored by accident, a contagious craze or fad, a chance demand for something of which scarcely the outside is known, —
all these whirr and buzz in every boyhood; but
to follow such superficial moods would mean the
dissolution of all organized life, and education
would be an empty word. Election which is
more than a chance grasping presupposes first of
all acquaintance with the object of our choice.
Even in the college two thirds of the elections are
haphazard, controlled by accidental motives ; elec-

tion of courses demands a wide view and broad
knowledge of the whole field. The lower the
level on which the choice is made, the more external and misleading are the motives which direct
it. A helter-skelter chase of the unknown is no
election. If a man who does not know French
goes into a restaurant where the bill of fare is
given in the French language, and points to one
line and to another, not knowing whether his
order is fish or roast or pudding, the waiter will
bring him a meal, but we cannot say that he has
" elected his courses."

From whatever standpoint I view it, the tendency to base the school on elective studies seems
to me a mistake, — a mistake for which, of course,
not a special school, but the social consciousness
is to be blamed. I cannot think much better of
that second tendency of which I spoke, — the
tendency to improve the schools by a pedagogic-
psychological preparation of the teachers. I said
that, just as I had no right of election over my
courses, my teachers did not base my education on
theories of pedagogy and psychology. I do not
think that they would have been better teachers
with such wisdom than without it. I doubt, even,
whether it would not have changed things for the
worse. I do not believe in lyrics which are written after the prescriptions of æsthetics; I have

the fullest respect for the scholar in poetical theory, but he ought not to make the poets believe that they need his advice before they dare to sing. Psychology is a wonderful science, and pedagogy, as soon as we shall have it, may be a wonderful science, too, and very important for school organizers, for superintendents and city officials, but the individual teacher has little practical use for it. I have discussed this point so often before the public that I am unwilling to repeat my arguments here. I have again and again shown that in the practical contact of the schoolroom the teacher can never gain that kind of knowledge of the child which would enable him to get the right basis for psychological calculation, and that psychology itself is unable to do justice to the demands of the individual case. I have tried to show how the conscious occupation with pedagogical rules interferes with instinctive views of right pedagogical means; and, above all, how the analytic tendency of the psychological and pedagogical attitude is diametrically opposite to that practical attitude, full of tact and sympathy, which we must demand of the real teacher; and that the training in the one attitude inhibits freedom in the other. And when I see that teachers sometimes interpret my warning as if I wished merely to say, " I, as a psychologist, dislike to

have any one approach the science with the purely
practical question whether it bakes bread, instead
of with a purely theoretical interest," I must object to that interpretation. I did not wish merely
to say that the bread question would better be de-
layed; no, the teacher ought to know from the
beginning that if he takes the bread which psychology bakes, indigestion must follow.

Yet I do not mean to be narrow. I do not
think that if teachers go through psychological
and pedagogical studies they will really suffer
very much; they will do with them what they do
with most studies, — they will forget them. And
if they forget them, what harm, then, — why all
this fighting against it, as if a danger were in
question? This brings me, finally, to my last but
chief point: I think, indeed, that great dangers
do exist, and that the psycho-pedagogical movement does serious damage, not so much because
it affects the teacher, but because it, together with
the enthusiasm for elective studies, turns the attention of the public from the only essential and
important point, upon which, I feel deeply convinced, the true reform of our schools is dependent, — the better instruction of our teachers.
That was the secret, I said, in our German
schools; the most elementary teaching was given
by men who were experts in their field, who had

the perspective of it, and whose scholarly interest
filled them with an enthusiasm that inspired the
class. To bring that condition about must be
the aim of every friend of American school life.
That is the one great reform which is needed, and
till this burning need is removed it is useless to
institute unimportant changes. These little pseu-
do-reforms become, indeed, a wrong, if they make
the public forget that true help and true reform
are demanded. If a child is crying because it is
ill, we may keep it quiet for a while by a piece of
candy, but we do not make it well; and it is a
wrong to quiet it, if its silence makes us omit to
call the physician to cure it. The elective studies
and the pedagogical courses are such sweetmeats
for education. The schools were bad, and the
public was dissatisfied; now the elective studies
relieve the discomfort of the children, in the place
of the old vexation they have a good time, and
the parents are glad that the drudgery is over.
And when, nevertheless, a complaint arises, and
the parents discover that the children do not learn
anything and that they become disrespectful, then
there comes the chance for the man with the psychological — and pedagogical — training; he is
not a better teacher, but he can talk about the
purposes of the new education till all is covered
by beautiful words; and thus parents and chil-

dren are happily satisfied for a while, till the time
comes when the nation has to pay for its neglect
in failing really to cure the sick child. Just as it
has been said that war needs three things, money,
money, and again money, so it can be said with
much greater truth that education needs, not forces
and buildings, not pedagogy and demonstrations,
but only men, men, and again men, — without for-
bidding that some, not too many of them, shall
be women.

The right kind of men is what the schools
need; they have the wrong kind. They need
teachers whose interest in the subject would banish
all drudgery, and they have teachers whose pitiable
unpreparedness makes the class work either so
superficial that the pupils do not learn anything,
or, if it is taken seriously, so dry and empty that
it is a vexation for children and teachers alike.
To produce anything equivalent to the teaching
staff from whose guidance I benefited in my boyhood, no one ought to be allowed to teach in a
grammar school who has not passed through a
college or a good normal school; no one ought to
teach in a high school who has not worked, after
his college course, at least two years in the graduate school of a good university; no one ought
to teach in a college who has not taken his doctor's degree in one of the best universities; and

no one ought to teach in a graduate school who
has not shown his mastery of method by powerful
scientific publications. We have instead a misery
which can be characterized by one statistical fact:
only two per cent of the schoolteachers possess
any degree whatever. If the majority of college
teachers are hardly prepared to teach in a secondary school, if the majority of high-school teachers
are hardly fit to teach in a primary school, and
if the majority of primary-school teachers are
just enough educated to fill a salesgirl's place in
a millinery store, then every other reform is self-
deceit.

I do not feel at all surprised that many of my
brethren who are seriously interested in the progress of education rush forward in the wrong
direction. They have been brought up under
the prescribed system, with teachers who did not
know pedagogy, and they feel instinctively that
the schools are bad and need reform. It is only
natural for them to think that the prescriptive
system is guilty, and that pedagogy can help us;
they are so filled with aversion to the old-fashioned school that they think only of the matter
which they were taught and the method after which
they were taught; but as they have no standard
of comparison in their own experience, they never
imagine that it may have been the men alone, the

teachers, who were responsible for the failures.
These friends have never experienced what my
classmates and I enjoyed, — prescribed courses
with expert teachers. They do not and cannot
imagine the revolution which comes into the
schoolroom as soon as a teacher stands on the
platform who has the inspiring enthusiasm for his
science which springs from a profound scholarly
knowledge. No pedagogical technique can be
substituted for this only real preparation of the
teacher ; and I fear that pedagogy must become
a hindrance to educational progress, if it ever
causes the principal or the school board to prefer
the teacher who has learned pedagogy to the
teacher who has learned the subject he is going
to teach.

My German memories, however, not only arouse
in me a pessimism with regard to those pseudo-
reforms ; they give me also most optimistic views
with regard to a point which may be raised as an
objection to my views. The teaching staff is bad
indeed, it has often been said, but how can we
hope for an improvement? The boys leave the
high school at eighteen years of age, the college
at twenty-two ; how can we hope that an average
high-school teacher will devote a still larger part
of his life to the preparation for his professional
work, and will spend two or three years more in

a graduate school before he begins to earn his living? This argument is utterly wrong, as it neglects the interrelation of the different factors. If we had thoroughly prepared teachers, the aims of the school would be reached here just as quickly as in Germany, where, as I have shown, the level of American high-school graduation is attained at fifteen years, and the level of average American college graduation at nineteen. Time which, with the teachers of to-day, is hardly sufficient to bring a man through a good high school would then be enough to give him a college education, and the time which to-day is necessary to pull him through college should be enough to give him three years in the graduate school. I was twenty-two when I took my doctor's degree in Leipzig, and so were most of my friends. The change cannot come suddenly; but as soon as the public recognizes in what direction true reform of education must lie, it can be brought about by a slow, persistent pushing along that line. If the schools insist more and more on the solid scholarship of the teachers, the time in which the ends of the school are reached will become shorter and shorter: this will give more and more room for the continuation of study on the part of the future teachers, and thus we should enter upon a beneficial revolution which would

in a short time supply the whole country with efficient teachers.   If we look at the situation from
this point of view, we can hardly doubt that even
those who have only the utilitarian interest in
mind, — yes, even those who think of the mercenary aspect only, — that even those must prefer this true reform to the efforts of the "new
education" men who operate with pedagogy and
elective studies.   Those three years which every
American boy loses through the bad preparation
of his teachers represent a loss for the practical
achievement in later life which cannot be compensated for by an early beginning of professional
training through electives.   It is a loss for the
man, and an incomparable loss for the nation.

I merely indicated one other feature of our
German education when I disclosed the secret of
its efficiency.   I said that our parents reinforced
in us respect for the school, and that the home
atmosphere was filled with belief in the duties of
school life.   Our parents did not need mothers'
clubs and committees for that, and there was little
discussion about what children need *in abstracto ;*
but they made their children feel that the home
and the school were working in alliance.   We
boys took all that as a matter of course, and what
it meant I never quite understood before I crossed
the ocean.   I feel inclined to say that what our

schoolchildren need is not only good teachers, but also good parents. They need fathers who feel the responsibility to be the ultimate moral guides of the youth and who do not undermine by carelessness the patient work of the teacher. They need mothers who through all their love and indulgence steadily insist on the seriousness of duties and who are not misled by the superficial theories of half-educated educators to believe that persuasion only and never command has to enter the nursery. They need parents who understand what they are doing when they keep their children at home from school on rainy days or let them omit the school work when guests are coming, when they allow their youngsters to be idle through the whole long vacations, when they urge the school to reduce and reduce the daily home work, and when they enjoy the jokes of the child on the teacher. It is a noble thing that Americans put millions into new schoolhouses, but to build up the education in the classroom without a foundation in the serious responsible aid of the parents, is not better than to build those magnificent buildings of brick and stone on shifting sand.

III

I

THE idea of continental Europe in regard to
the productive scholars of the New World can be
as easily as briefly stated : there is none. A widely
read German history of civilization says this about
American scholarship : " American universities
are hardly more than ordinary schools in Germany.
It is true, they receive large sums of money from
rich men ; but they cannot attain to anything,
because the institutions either remain under the
control of the church, or the professors are appointed on account of their political or personal
connections, not on account of their knowledge.
The professors therefore have, naturally, more
interest in money-making than in the advancement of science. Not a single one of these institutions has reached a scientific position." And
if this expresses the opinion of the public at large,
it must be admitted that the scholars are seldom
much better informed. They see hundreds of
American students migrating to Germany every
year, and feel sure that they would not come in

such streams if America had anything of comparable value to offer. American publications cross the ocean in a ridiculously small number; in the world of letters no Columbus has yet discovered the other side of the globe.

Is it necessary to defend myself against the suspicion that I share this European prejudice? I have my witnesses in print. Since I resigned my German professorship to enter Harvard University, I have heartily welcomed every opportunity to write for German readers about my delightful surprises in the academic world here, and about the contrast between the facts here and the fables current over there. Last summer I had a glorious opportunity. A well-known naturalist of Switzerland, whose opinions are often heard in German magazines, came here for scientific purposes, and spent his vacation in various places. When he returned, he gathered his impressions in an essay published in the most widely read review, and condensed his opinions on American universities as follows: "The American universities are of unequal value; some are simply humbug. They are all typically American, illustrating in every respect the American spirit: they have an essentially practical purpose. The American wishes to see quick returns in facts and successes; he has scarcely ever any comprehension

of theory and real science. He has not yet had
time to understand that scholarly truth is like a
beautiful woman, who should be loved and honored for her own sake, while it is a degradation
to value her only for her practical services : a
Yankee brain of to-day cannot grasp that," —
and so on. I published at once in the same magazine an extended reply. I demonstrated therein
how easily the foreigner is misled by the use of
the word " university " for institutions which are
nothing but colleges, and that, therefore, a fair
comparison with German universities is possible
only for the dozen institutions which are adjusted
to postgraduate work. I pointed out that in these
leading universities the opportunities offered students are not inferior to those abroad ; that the
theoretical courses, not the practical ones, are
favored by the students ; and that, especially in
unpractical fields, as astronomy, geology, eth-
nology, Sanskrit, English philology, philosophy,
very valuable work has been done. I claimed with
full conviction that the doctor's degree of our
best universities is superior to the average degree
in Germany, and that our libraries and equip-
ments are not seldom better than those on the
other side. I showed with enthusiasm what an
increasing number of scholarly magazines is sent
out by our institutions, how great is the output

of new books in every field, how the academies and scholarly associations flourish. Yes, I became pathetic, and sentimental, and ironical, and enthusiastic, and my friends maintained that I made my point; and yet in my heart I was glad that no one raised the other question, whether I really believed that American scholarship is to-day all that it ought to be. I should have felt obliged to confess that I did not; and as I speak now to Americans only, I may add here all that I forgot to tell my German readers.

I do not want to disclaim a single word of my German plea for the American world of learning. The situation is infinitely better than Europeans suppose it to be, — in certain branches of knowledge excellent work has been done; and yet I am convinced that the result stands in no proper proportion to the achievements of American culture in all the other aspects of national life, a fact which the best American scholars everywhere frankly acknowledge and seriously deplore. Yes, America now has scholarship, as well as Germany; but it is just as when the Germans claim that they, as well as the Americans, play football, — they do play it, to be sure, but in cutaways and high collars. Many Americans consider that there is nothing amiss with the condition of scholarship here, and some are even proud of it;

a nation which has to " do " things ought not to
care much for knowledge.   But there are others
who see the dangers of such an attitude.   They
believe that there is no ideal of learning and
searching for truth which is too high for the
American nation.   They think, as Emerson said,
that " our days of dependence, our long appren-
ticeship to the learning of other lands draws to
a close ; the millions that around us are rushing
into life cannot always be fed on the remains of
foreign harvests."   And as the first necessary
condition of such a change they seek a clear insight into the causes which lie at the root of this
shortcoming.   To these it may perhaps appear not
quite useless to try to throw light on those causes
from the standpoint of a comparison between the
American and the German conditions for productive scholarship.

In America, as in Germany, the question of
productive scholarship is essentially a university
question, as in both countries the chief advancers
of knowledge have been at the same time professional daily teachers of academic youth.   This
relation is in itself not at all necessary, and certainly does not hold true for other countries, such
as France and England.   In England and in
France, a great part of the finest scholarly work
has been done by men who had no relations to

academic institutions; and if they filled university positions, their rôle was, on the whole, a decorative one, while the real daily teaching was done by minor men. Here, as in Germany, the union of scholar and teacher in one person is the rule ; the scholars who are not teachers are in both countries the exception. I do not overlook the fact that such exceptional cases exist on both sides ; historians like Rhodes, Fiske, Lodge, Roosevelt, and others stand outside of academic life. A similar situation is occupied by some economists and some naturalists, especially those connected with the government institutions in Washington ; there are physicians and inventors, lawyers and ministers, who aim, outside of the institutions of learning, toward real advancement of knowledge, and yet they form here, exactly as over there, such a small minority that they do not determine the character of the scholarship of the country, while in England and France they are its most important factor. Here, too, the work of the outsiders will be measured by the standards set by the universities. Every advantage and disadvantage, every reform and every danger for scholarship, is in America, therefore, as in Germany, first of all a university problem.

To give to our inquiry narrower limits, I shall omit from consideration the law school, medical school, and divinity school. The law schools especially are, on account of the differences of law, so absolutely unlike here and abroad that they may be totally eliminated. If we thus confine ourselves, on the whole, to the humanistic and scientific studies, to philology and history, economics and philosophy, literature and the fine arts, mathematics and physics, biology and chemistry and geology, and so on, we compare similar matters. And on this basis now arises the question at issue : Why has Germany's productive scholarship attained the power to mould the thoughts of the world, while America's, so far, has not ? Why are the German universities such fertile ground that in them even the smallest talent comes to flower, and the American universities such sterile ground that here often the finest energies are destined to wither ?

II

One reason offers itself at once : in Germany, the very idea of a university demands productive scholarship as the centre and primary interest of all university activity ; in America it is essentially an accessory element, a secondary factor, almost a luxury, which is tolerated, but never demanded as a condition. But this fact itself has deeper reasons, and we must understand the whole spirit

of the universities there and here to understand
why it is so, and why it must be so under the
conditions that obtain to-day. In Germany, the
spirit of the university is absolutely different from
that of the preceding stage, the gymnasium; in
America, the university work is mostly a continuation of the college work, without any essential
qualitative difference. The postgraduate work is
more difficult than the undergraduate work, the
teachers are expected to know more, the subjects
are more advanced and specialized; but all the
changes are of quantitative character, and there
is nothing new in principle. The university is
a more difficult college, — a college which presupposes a greater amount of information, and where
the best informed teachers of the country are
teaching; but its spirit is on the whole the college spirit, merely on a more elaborate scale of
instruction.

In Germany, there is no greater difference than
exists between the spirit of the university period
and that of the school time. The gymnasium furnishes education and information; the university
brings to the younger generation the scholarly,
scientific spirit. The gymnasium distributes the
knowledge which has been collected; the university teaches the student to take a critical attitude
toward all collected knowledge. The gymnasium

teaches facts and demands text-books; the university teaches method and presupposes all that can be found in books by independent study. The gymnasium gives to the boy of nineteen nothing different in principle from what the boy of nine receives; the university offers to the student of twenty something absolutely different from what he received a year before. The teacher of the gymnasium must, therefore, be a man who has learned a great deal, and has a talent for imparting what he has learned; the teacher of the university must be a master of method. But there is only one test to prove that a man has mastered the methods of a science: he must have shown that he is able to advance it. The teacher of the university is, therefore, above all, a productive scholar, while to the gymnasium teacher productive scholarship is something non-essential.

This higher type of institution, this qualitatively new principle of instruction, has thus far not been completely realized in America. I am speaking, of course, of the ideal and of the theory. In practice, there are many German university professors whose lectures run down to mere schoolteaching, and there are many brilliant American professors whose invaluable scholarly lectures and research courses are fully inspired by the highest university ideal. But while the former simply do

not fulfill their duty, and remain below the level
of public expectation, the latter transcend the official and generally accepted ideal of university life.
The official ideal of the American university is, as
it has been expressed with emphasis, an institution
in which " everybody can learn everything." And
yet nothing is further removed than this from
the ideal of that other university where not every
one is admitted as a student, but only the one who
has reached a maturity in which he can go over
from mere learning to criticism; and where not
everything is to be learned, but one thing alone,
the highest intellectual grasp of the scholarly
spirit. A young man who is mature enough to
enter the university ought to be able to learn
" everything " for himself; but the method of
dealing with anything, not as a fact, but as a
problem, he can gain only from a master. The
college may teach " things ; " the graduate school
ought to teach the stating of problems. The
college teaches dogmatically ; the graduate school
ought to train in critical thinking. The college
is for intellectual boys; the university ought to
be for intellectual manhood ; as the college makes
the students dependent upon the authorities,
while the university ought to teach them to be
self-dependent, to stand on their own feet.

This is the point where American intellectual

culture betrays its limitations : American institutions do not show sufficient insight into the fundamental fact that the highest kind of knowledge is not wide, but self-dependent. Yes, Americans, who are so proud of their spirit of initiative and independence, too often overlook the fact that the highest independence of character can go hand in hand with the most slavish intellectual dependence, and that all which is merely "learned," all text-book information, all knowledge without mastery of method, is good for boys, but poor for intellectual men. And yet such a self-dependent attitude is never the result of a mere skeptical incredulity or of defiant contradiction of the authorities, but can be gained only by the fullest training in methodological criticism. No one, even in his special field, can really examine everything himself, but he is not self-dependent till he fully knows how to do it ; that is, till at least in one point he has proved to himself that he is able to go beyond all that mankind has hitherto known about it. If he is able to master the methods for one problem, then he has the power to do so for others ; he may now follow a leader, but he knows that he does not follow simply because there is a chain on his leg which pulls him along. No amount of information can be substituted for training, and a university course which

deals with the history of ten years from a really
critical point of view is therefore more important
than another which pictures a thousand years
from a dogmatic standpoint. Self-dependence in
knowledge thus never means ignoring the authorities, and even in the natural sciences does not
come from a direct appeal to Nature, as the science
teachers of the schools too often believe. Nature
answers always only those questions which we ask
her ; and the whole history of science — that is, the
authorities — must teach us first how to ask our
questions of Nature. Self-dependence means the
power to understand the authorities, and to deal
with them critically.

As I have said, the only possible teacher for
this highest kind of intellectual activity must be
a scholar who is himself a master of scientific
method, and as such a master only is the productive scholar tested. That is the reason why productive scholarship is the very informing spirit of
German universities, and why no teacher is ever
appointed as university docent who has not proved
his power over methods by publications which
have at some point advanced human knowledge.
Productive scholarship will never reach a really
high level in America till it becomes the informing spirit of the American universities also; and
it cannot be their spirit till the difference between

the ideal of the university and the ideal of the college, between the critical and the dogmatic attitude in knowledge, is fully grasped by the community. As long as the university is essentially a better equipped college on a more elaborate scale, the appointment of university teachers must be determined by the same considerations that influence the usual choice of a college teacher. As it is, — given, of course, the moral qualities, — a man is sought who has learned much about his subject and is an efficient teacher. But whether he has produced anything of scholarly value is, on the whole, a secondary question.

The situation in our colleges is similar to that in the German gymnasiums. The gymnasium teacher is not at all unproductive. Most of his productions, to be sure, are just as in the colleges here, merely text-books; but many gymnasium teachers publish scholarly investigations, and as almost every one has written his doctor's thesis, many go on with their productive university studies; some have published excellent books. And yet their publications are in a way their private affairs, not their official duty; their professional work can be conceived as complete without any effort in that direction; there are even principals of gymnasiums who look with a certain suspicion on the too productive teacher, because they are afraid that he may neglect his class duties, or may raise the level of instruction too high for the pupils. But in any case, if productive scholarship were in the hands of these gymnasium teachers only, science and scholarship would be the same lukewarm affair that it is here in the hands of college men, — a professional luxury, relegated to the scarce leisure hours of an overworked man who has little to gain from it, and whose career and professional standing are hardly influenced thereby.

How different the university man, if university instruction is rightly understood as the teaching of method, of criticism, of self-dependence ! What other way is open to prove the possession of a power than the use — and the successful use — of it ? A singer who does not sing, a painter who does not paint, and a university scholar who does not advance human knowledge, stand then on exactly the same level. Of course it is not necessary that the productive work should appear directly under the name of the author; here, as in Germany, some of the finest scholars put forth their thoughts through the publications of their advanced students, for whose work they take the responsibility. But if the instructor does not publish in one way or another, directly or indirectly, theoretical assurances will not suffice. To say that a man might have advanced human knowledge, if he had not preferred to give all his time to teaching by lectures or by popular books and articles, is absurd, if he never had an opportunity to be tried. He might just as well say that he would have been skillful in walking the tight rope, if he had not preferred his life long to walk on the floor. The fact that he is a good teacher has, of course, no bearing on the point. If we want to find a man who is a master of critical methods, we cannot be satisfied if the man shows that he has much information, and skill in imparting it. For that we need the original mind, while the merely imitative thinker may make a most excellent teacher. Any one who has a personality, a forcible way of presentation, and an average intellect will be able to be a fine teacher of any subject at six weeks' notice. The student cannot judge whether the thoughts brought forward in the lecture are the instructor's own thoughts or a rehash of the contents of half a dozen text-books; or even if they are his own thoughts, whether they have any legs to stand on. Whether the teacher's thoughts are cheap reproductions or valuable critical studies can be determined only by a jury of his peers, and the only way to communicate with them is by publications. The teacher's papers and books alone decide

whether he is or is not in possession of that power
of scholarly grasp which the university student
is to learn from him, and thus whether he is or is
not fit to be a university teacher.

III

No one ought to interpret this to mean a lack
of appreciation for the receptive scholarship and
the fine teaching qualities of a good college instructor who wants to be a teacher only, or a
writer of pleasant and helpful popular books. I
do not at all claim that his function is less noble,
or that his achievement is less important for the
community, and I know, of course, that " distribution" of knowledge is not at all an easy or a
mechanical task when it is well done; the really
good teacher needs many gifts and qualities which
may be absent in great scholars. I maintain
merely that the two professions are different, —
as different as that of the photographer from that
of the artist. A good photographer is certainly
a more useful being than a bad artist; but no
photographer understands the meaning of art who
thinks that he and Sargent are in principle doing
the same thing. As long as. productive scholarship is not recognized by the public consciousness
as something absolutely different from receptive
scholarship, its development must remain an acci-

dental one, and can never reach the level which American civilization has reached in so many other directions, and which might be expected from the large external resources of the higher institutions of learning. That the outcome in important work is disappointing, no one can deny ; nor will any one seriously doubt that the ignorance of Europe in regard to American work will disappear rapidly as soon as really fundamental work is done. As soon as a Darwin or a Helmholtz, a Virchow or a Bunsen, a Spencer or a Pasteur or a Mommsen speaks in the smallest New England college, the whole world will find him out and listen ; but he must speak, as his European colleagues have spoken, in the service of productive scholarship only, while he will remain unheard if he follows the leadings of his surroundings, becomes merely a good teacher, writes text-books and magazine essays and popular lectures.

There is another point on which I must not be misunderstood. In Germany, the gymnasium, as the place of receptive scholarship, and the university, as the place where the productive scholar teaches critical method, are sharply separated. I do not mean that this external separation is in itself necessary, or, under American conditions, either desirable or possible. Such a complete separation can be made only where the government guarantees an equality of standard, and where conditions are equal throughout the land. In the United States, the system of sliding scales, of infinitesimal differences, of transitions from low forms to higher ones without sharp lines of demarcation, has shown itself to be the soundest in all educational matters; the smallest institution must have the possibility of growing up to the highest requirements, and each local foundation must be able to adapt itself to special needs. In a country where the greatest educational progress comes through private initiative and through the slow raising of the standards of requirements in the social consciousness, the system of sliding transitions offers the best chance for healthful development; and the raising of the graduate schools to the plane of real universities can come only as the fruit of such a system, just as the present graduate school has developed itself naturally by that system out of the average college. What is necessary is only the development of the new ideal in the social mind. On the other hand, so long as the real principle is not acknowledged, the mere imitation of external forms or the artificial construction of new schemes cannot bring about an improvement. For instance, the dropping of the college department represents no progress at all, if the remainder is in itself on no

higher level than the average graduate school.
The claim of an institution that it is in the lead
because it has no college is without basis as long
as its teachers are in no way superior, as productive scholars, to the average instructors of other
universities. The omission of the lower forms is
no gain, and has at present great disadvantages.
I do not believe that the development of the
highest forms is to be expected along this line.
I remember I once saw in the far West two insignificant institutions in the same county. One
called itself, modestly, a college; the other, a
university. As I saw clearly that the university
was lower in its standards of graduation, I asked
the director about the designation; and he
answered that they called themselves a university
because they were of so much higher grade than
the neighboring college. I asked him in what
respect they were of higher grade, as they had no
graduate school, no law school, and no medical
school. " No," he said, " we have not all these,
but we are higher because we have no preparatory school."

The functions of the student stand, of course,
in immediate relation to the functions of the
instructor. If the instructor gives information,
the student is expected to learn facts; and he shows
best by examinations whether or not he has suc-

ceeded. If the task of the instructor is to teach
the method of scholarly criticism, the student
aims at getting a scholarly grasp ; and whether or
not he has succeeded he can prove only by showing that in one little point, at least, he can advance
human knowledge. Original research then becomes the backbone of his university work, and
the publication of a doctor's thesis its natural
goal. This aspect of student's work grows
among us from year to year, and yet it has not
won sufficient strength to stand alone against all
attacks. There are still institutions which do
their research work as a concession to a doubtful
fashion, imported from Germany, and necessary
as an advertisement in the struggle of university
competition ; there is still a majority which does
not believe in it at all ; and there are still leading
universities here which do not require the printing of the doctor's thesis. It is a very curious
fact that the most effective argument brought forward here again and again, in the fight against
the doctor's thesis, is the cheap scholarship of
many of the German doctor-dissertations. At the
basis of this there is a misunderstanding, as the
German doctor's thesis cannot be compared with
the American one. In Germany the doctor-examination is, on the whole, a purely decorative affair
for the gaining of a title which has not the slight-

est consequence for the career of a man, but only
the social value of a personal address. All open-
ings to the career of teacher, as well as to that of
lawyer or physician, are dependent on the very severe state examination, which shows clearly whether
or not the candidate has acquired the scientific view
of his subjects. The man who has passed the
state examination may thus pass with a low mark
the doctor-examination, even if he presents merely
a hasty, superficial piece of research, just to satisfy traditional regulations. As the degree has
no practical bearing, and as it is always given
with one of four marks, there is no danger in
sometimes letting the thesis work run down. In
America, however, the doctor-examination is the
one goal of the post-graduate studies; it is the
one entrance gate to the best positions; and it
has thus the function of the German doctorate
together with that of the German state examination. The small group of men for whom the doctor's degree in Germany has a practical bearing
is the circle of those who enter the university
career; that is, those who seek to become privat-
docents of a university, and not teachers of a
gymnasium. The entrance on a university career
is indeed dependent on the " doctor " only, and
not on the state examination; but for this purpose it is required to gain the doctor's degree

with one of the two highest marks, and no thesis
which has been marked with *summa* or *magna
cum laude* is of that cheap kind of unthinking
research which is so often shown here as a dread-
ful example.   Only these excellent theses can thus
be fairly compared with those in question for
American universities, and they are certainly of a
kind to encourage production and publication.

But more than that.   Even if the dissertations
were in themselves valueless for human knowledge, if they were unworthy of publication, if
they were unnecessary as tests for the students,
original research, with the goal of a definite
special problem to be settled by really scientific
methods, would continue to be nowhere more
needed than here, as the one great stimulus which
our graduates get to active scholarly interest.   In
Germany they find these incentives through all
their lives, in a hundred forms; here everything
comes together to work in the other direction,
and to keep men away from the really scientific attitude.   The small tasks of original research of the students in the university time
are the little fountains in the woods, whose waters
unite in the brook which is seen by the world;
and only if they are plentiful will the brook ever
become a river.   It is well known that the beginnings of productive scholarship in this country,

thirty or forty years ago, were due to those who came home from such research work in German universities, and that these beginnings have been reinforced and developed by the hundreds who have gone abroad for their studies during the last decades, till only recently the time has come when the American graduate can find the same opportunities in the best American universities. These stimulations of the student time are the real influences which will decide the future of American scholarship ; and whoever belittles the value and retards the development of the students' research and of the doctorate must understand that he is helping to destroy the real scholarship of the country, or to make it dependent upon that of other nations. At present there seems no occasion to fear for the standard of the degree ; the standard is kept high, but the number of those who seek it is far too small. No one who intends to teach in a college, or even in a high school, ought to end his academic years before he has attained the degree. He has not, like the university teacher, to teach the methods of scholarship, and, therefore, is under no necessity to lead the life of a productive scholar, but the spark of active scholarship must have touched him ; if he has remained throughout merely a receptive scholar, merely a good college boy, even with his Master of Arts, his teaching will be sterile drudgery.

IV

I have said that after the student days everything militates against scholarly production, in this country ; that our young man enters into a world which does not care for his original work. No one can understand the conditions of productive scholarship here who does not consider the path which our young scholar has to follow. I have at present in my psychological seminary at Harvard twenty-six advanced graduate students, — on the average better prepared for scholarly work than the members of a seminary in a German university, as the men here are more mature from their more advanced age, and as the stricter regulation of attendance and course-examinations has laid a larger basis of information. What can I now hope from these young men with regard to their chances of making use of their scholarly power in the next twenty years, compared with the chances which just such a set of young men would have in Germany ? Over there, the best of them, the more talented ones, the more ambitious ones, and, I may at once add, the socially stronger ones would choose the career of productive scholarship ; and while the majority would be satisfied to jog along the road of the gymnasium teacher, doing the prescribed daily work,

without any original effort, some would enter the
university career as privat-docents. There might
be only three or four in such a group who were
ready to do so, but no instructor would feel dis-
appointed if he knew that there was at least one
among his students in whom the seed would bring
fruit. Once admitted to the university as such
privat-docents, they can teach as much as they
want to, and, above all, can teach whatever they
choose, even the most specialized topic in which
they are interested ; they live in an academic
atmosphere, devoted exclusively to productive
thought, and so they wait till a vacancy of a professorship occurs, knowing that it will be filled
by the man who has done the most valuable piece
of scholarly work. Their whole ambition is thus
directed toward the advancement of science. Of
course the choice has to be made by men, and
thus human prejudices and passions must enter.
It is not always the best scholar who gets the
place, — cliques and parties obscure the ideal
there as everywhere ; but at least the principle is
safe, and certainly a local candidate has no advantage over any one else, for the outlook covers
all docents who have entered the arena of scholarly literature. And further, while in democratic
America the appointments are made by the president and by the trustees of the institutions, with-

out the official coöperation of the faculty, in monarchical Germany no government can appoint a
professor who has not been proposed by the faculty, — that is, by the professional scholars, who
have no more important interest than that of
keeping high, by their coöperation, the level of
productive scholarship in their university. All
the academic premiums await there the young
scholar who develops his scientific powers, and
thus the institution of docents becomes the real
backbone of German university work.

How different here! Our young men, when
they have left our research courses, some of them
with a fresh Ph. D. degree in their pockets, have
no other prospect before them than to enter into
a college as instructors. I do not speak of those
who choose another profession, become perhaps
school superintendents or technical specialists;
nor do I speak of those whose work was not satis-
factory enough to secure them a college position,
and who must be contented with lower school
positions. I speak of the best, — those who get
all our blessings in the form of superlative letters to teachers' agencies and college presidents.
Even these are satisfied when they get decent instructorships or assistant professorships in a college; and they are delighted if the college is by
chance not too remote in the Southwest, and

if it is not so denominational that they have to sacrifice their convictions, and if it is not so deep in debt that half of the promised salary cannot be paid on time. Let us take, again, the best cases. A good man goes into a good college. We all know what he has to expect.

He finds an abundance of work, which crushes by its quantity his good will to go on with scholarly interests. The young man who has to conduct twenty " recitations " a week, and to read hundreds of examination books, and to help on the administrative life of his place, begins by postponing his scientific work to the next year, and the year after next, when he shall be more accustomed to his duties. But after postponing it for a few years more his will becomes lame, his power rusty, his interest faded. The amount of work, however, seems to me the least important issue, and I think it a mistake to regard it as the chief obstacle to production. After all, the day has twenty-four hours, and the year has fifty-two weeks; a young man with full vitality can carry a heavy burden. I have known men who taught more than twenty hours weekly, and yet considered the teaching as filling the leisure hours between the periods of real work, which was their scholarly production. Much more essential seems to me the quality of the duties. A young scholar

ought to devote himself to special problems,
where he can really go to the sources : instead of
that, our young instructor has to devote himself
to the widest fields, where it is impossible to aim
at anything but the most superficial acquaintance.
The experienced master can remain scholarly even
when he gives the general elementary courses ;
the beginner, who has no chance ever to focus on
one point, but must all the time teach merely the
outlines of his subject, will quickly sink to a
cheap undignified interpretation.   At first he is
troubled in his scholarly conscience, remembering
the spirit of the graduate school ; but soon he
grows accustomed to the prostitution of science,
shame disappears, he gets to be satisfied with a
method of thinking which makes his courses
effective and his work easy, and the possibility of
his own production fades out of sight.   And he
has plenty of excuses on his lips : the library of
his college is so poor ; his small laboratory gives
him no opportunity ; his salary is too meagre to
let him buy books for himself.   Above all, he
wants to earn a little additional money.   Scholarly papers in scientific magazines are not paid
for.   But several convenient roads are open.
He may write a short text-book ; as the students
must buy it, the publisher can pay for it.   Now
the scholar knows that there is nothing more dif-

ficult and nothing more easy than to write text-books. The great scholar, who has tried his power in scores of special investigations, may try, at the height of his work, to connect his thoughts about the whole field into one system, and to translate it into the simple terms of a book for beginners. That is the sort of text-book which helps the world, — nothing is more difficult and more noble; every line written therein stands for pages. But if a beginner comes and adds to twenty text-books the twenty-first, it is scientific reporter work, enervating and ruinous for the scholarly seriousness of the author. Another way is that of popular lectures — preferably before women's clubs — and articles for popular magazines. All that is poison for the beginner, who loses increasingly the power to discriminate between what is solid and what is for effect, as he moves away from the criticism of scholars, and addresses audiences which applaud every catchy phrase.

Yet the young sufferer who has all these motives as his conscious excuses, and who thinks that he could do original work if he had less lecturing and more money, is mostly unconscious of the strongest factor which pulls him down, as it is a negative factor, which is felt merely by comparison with the situation abroad. This negative

factor is the absence of a decided premium upon
scholarly production. If he is a fine man, with
vitality, he wants to get on ; the safest way is to
climb up in his own institution, since the possibility of being called to other places depends
largely upon chance. But in any case here the
advancements and the appointments are made
almost without any reference to original production. The men who busy themselves with administrative troubles, who are favorites with the
elementary students, who are pleasant speakers,
who show themselves industrious by manufactur-
ing books for class use, win the premiums in the
competition. And all these are merely the ideal
factors : there are plenty of factors the reverse of
ideal working besides. Yes, with the exception of
the leading universities, the young scholar sees
productive work so lightly valued that he must
consider it a very unsafe investment of energy ;
and if his passionate zeal and ardent delight in
searching out truth hold him fast to the path of
scholarship, he feels dimly that he is damaging
his chances with the trustees of his little college,
and thus, in the majority of cases, working
against his own interest. What can be expected
from the productive output of a young generation
laboring under such conditions, compared with
the possibilities in Germany, where in the twenty-

one universities more than seven hundred privat-
docents are at present working, every one of whom
adjusts his teaching to his pleasure, — perhaps
one or two hours a week on a subject in which he
is absorbed; every one of whom has no other
ambition, and really no other hope, than to draw
the attention of the scholarly public to his scholarly productions, knowing that he loses his chance
for advancement if he indulges in superficialities?
It is just on account of this period of trial which
lies before our young doctors that it becomes so
essential to require the printing of the doctor's
thesis. That little printed sheet has once for all
brought the beginner before the scholarly world;
and while his daily work belongs to his unappre-
ciative surroundings, his intimate interests connect
him in his lonely place with the great outer world
of truth-seekers. He follows up the magazines to
see the traces of his little publication, he remains
interested to defend his budding theory, he goes on
to develop the incomplete parts of it; and thus
his dissertation becomes the one thread which
binds him in his days of instructorship to the
ideals of his graduate-student time.

But let us take for comparison the most favorable case under our conditions. Our young man
is vigorous and successful; he becomes a professor
in a real university after ten or twenty years. Is

he there finally in an atmosphere where the greatest possible output of all that his energies allow is encouraged by the conditions of the institution? Of course the situation is now more favorable for his serious work than in the small college, — the standard is much higher, the atmosphere more dignified; the outer means for work, books, instruments, are plentiful; advanced students are ready to follow him; his teaching is reduced to a very reasonable amount, — perhaps one or two hours a day. Everything seems encouraging, and yet he feels instinctively that the fullest stimulus which he had hoped for is even here not found; he feels as if, under other conditions, more might be attained with his energies; yes, even here it is as if he had to do his productive work, in a way, against outer influences which pull him back.

I return therewith to the point whence I started. Our friend who has successfully found his way from the little college to the university finds, perhaps with surprise, that, after all, here, too, at all decisive points, the college spirit overcomes the university spirit; that the whole academic community is controlled by the ideal of the perfect distribution of knowledge, and not by respect for productive scholarship and the imparting of method. He sees that the vital forces here also

are the good teachers, and not the great thinkers. He sees himself, perhaps, in a faculty where
real scholars mingle with men who have not the
slightest ambition to advance human knowledge,
but who have simply done on a great scale all
that the men in his fresh-water college did on
a narrow scale. He feels as if his productive
scholarship were merely tolerated, or at least considered unessential, as no one demands it from
the others as an essential condition of their presence. How surprised he is when he sees the
alumni of the university meet, and listens to their
speeches in praise of the alma mater! He hears
beautiful words about patriotism and liberal education, about athletics and gifts of money, about
the glorious history and the gifted sons who have
become men of public affairs; but that the university is a place for productive scholarship he does
not hear mentioned. He had thought that the
advances of human knowledge by the members of
his university were the milestones in its history,
like the battles which a regiment has fought; he
had thought that, as in Germany, the great scholarly conquests of the members of the faculties
were the common pride of the old students; and
now he sees that here, too, no one officially values his cherished ideals. They still remain his
private luxury, apart from human ambition and

social premiums. And his greatest disappoint-
ment comes when he sees that even here the activity of productive scholarship adjusts itself to the
financial situation, and that all the material conditions push the teachers away from productive
scholarship just as strongly in the large university as in the little college where the instructor
was paid like a car conductor.

V

Whenever in Greek-letter societies, among sol-
emn speeches, some one makes an academic oration
about the profession of the scholar, one feature
is never forgotten : the scholar does not care for
money. That sounds certainly very uplifting,
but it seems hardly true to any one who sees how
the great majority of American professors seek
money-making opportunities that have a varnish
of scholarship, but no pretense of scholarly aims.
In a hundred forms, of course, the temptation
comes, and by a hundred means does it creep into
the scholar's life, to absorb every hour of leisure
which ought to belong to purely ideal pursuits.
He will not do anything that will bring money,
but he will do few things that bring no money;
and as the really scholarly books never bring any
income, he deceives himself by all kinds of compromises, — writes popular books here and arti-

cles for an encyclopædia there, makes schoolbooks
and writes expert's testimonials, works in university extension and lectures before audiences whose
judgment he despises. Some energetic men can
stand all that without the slightest injury to their
higher work; for the greater number it means
surrender as productive scholars. And yet it is
all justified; unjustified alone is the social situation which forces upon a serious scholar such self-
destructive activity, and unjustified is the procla-
mation of the maxim that the scholar ought not to
care for a better material fate.

To be sure, it is most honorable in a scholar to
accept such a situation in dignified silence; but
often, while it is bad to speak about a thing, it
may be worse not to speak about it. It must be
said in all frankness that a financial situation in
which America's best scholars — that is, those
who are called to instructorships of the leading
universities — are so poorly paid that they feel
everywhere pushed into pursuits antagonistic to
scholarship, thus crushing the spirit of productive scholarship, is not only an undignified state
of things, but one of the greatest dangers to the
civilization of the country. The scholar is not to
be reproached as a greedy materialist for yielding.
As long as the present situation of scholarship
holds, the overwhelming majority of those who

go into teaching will have only narrow private means, and yet they will seek a comfortable life, and they ought to seek it as a background for creative work. They do not envy the rich banker his yachts and horses and diamonds, but they want a home of æsthetic refinement, they want excellent education for their children, they want a library well supplied, they want pleasant social intercourse and refreshing summer life and comfortable travel; and they ought to have all that without doing more than their normal university teaching, being thus free to devote the essential part of their time and thought to the advancement of productive scholarship. Exactly that is the situation in Germany, and no similar freedom of mind can be reached here by the scholar if every university professor, called to his place for real university work, has not a salary which corresponds to the income of the leading professors abroad. But to reproduce the benefits of the German situation and its influence on scientific production, it is not enough to raise the level of salaries; it is, above all, desirable to stop the mechanical equality which exists here generally, and which shows most clearly that, administratively, the American university still stands fairly under the ideal of the old college type, where the schoolman reigns and the scholar is a stranger.

The raising of the level of salaries may free the mind of the scholar from the search for opportunities to earn money, and thus from the corrupting influence of pseudo-scholarly temptations, but it is clearly a negative factor only; the inequality of salaries is a positive stimulus, provided that the highest salaries are really given to secure the services of the greatest scholars. In Germany, it not seldom happens that the income of one member of the faculty is five times larger than that of a colleague. There the school-teachers of the gymnasium have equal salaries, and their income grows according to seniority. That is entirely suitable, and a college cannot do otherwise. But to apply that principle to the valuation of scholarly production seems to the Germans not more logical than to fix the prices for all portrait painters according to the square inches of their canvas and their years of service. With them, many professors have much higher incomes than the highest officers of the state, who are their administrative superiors. Germany would never have reached that leading position in scholarship which is hers if she had treated her scholars like clerks or school-teachers, for whom the demand and supply can regulate the price mechanically, because the demand exists as a necessary one. The demand for higher scholarship has to be developed, and the supply has thus to be furthered beyond the present demand by a protective policy.

But America needs to offer large, even very large salaries on still another ground. The freeing of the scholar's mind from financial cares, and the stimulation of his productive energies, by a system which gives the highest rewards to the best scholarly work, the New World would share with the Old; but there is a third reason, which holds for America alone. It is to my mind the most important; and I confess that I should not have cared to touch the difficult salary problem at all if this point, which will decide the future of American scholarship, were not involved. We need high salaries, because at present they offer the only possible way to give slowly to productive scholarship social recognition and social standing, and thus to draw the best men of the land. Without great social premiums America will never get first-rate men as rank and file in the university teaching staff; and with second-rate men productive scholarship which is really productive for the world can never be created.

The greater number of those who devote themselves to higher teaching in America are young men without means, too often, also, without breeding; and yet that would be easily compensated for if they were men of the best minds, but

they are not. They are mostly men with a
passive, almost indifferent sort of mind, without
intellectual energy, men who see in the academic
career a modest, safe path of life, — exactly the
kind of men who in Germany become gymnasium
teachers. But those who in Germany become
docents of the university are for the most part of
the opposite type; they are, on the whole, the
best human material which the country has.
They come mostly from well-to-do families, and
seek the career because they feel the productive
mental energy and the ambition to try their
chances in a field of honor. Indeed, while the
profession of the gymnasium teacher stands in the
social estimation of the German below that of the
lawyer and the physician, the banker and the
wholesale merchant, the high respect of the German for productive science and art brings it about
that the profession of the university teacher, together with the aristocratic professions of officer
and diplomat, stands as the most highly esteemed
socially. Titles and decorations, as symbolic
forms of public appreciation, add another to the
outer stimulants to the greatest efforts. Thus the
social honor of the career, the large income, and,
above all, the delights of a life devoted purely to
the clean enjoyment of production, work together
to draw into the nets of the universities the very

best human material; and as, after all, personality is everywhere the decisive factor, the high quality of this human material secures the immense success of the work.

Nothing similar stands as yet as a temptation before the mind of the young American, and it would be to ignore the nature of man to believe that while all social premiums, all incentives for ambition and hopes, are absent, a merely theoretical interest will turn the youth to a kind of life which offers so little attraction. Can we really expect many brilliant young men of good families to enter a career which will for years demand from them superficial teaching in the atmosphere of a little college, with no hope, even in the case of highest success, of a salary equal to the income of a mediocre lawyer, and in a professional atmosphere in which the spirit of scholarly interest is suppressed by the spirit of school education? Our best young men must rush to law and banking, and what not. The type of man who in Germany goes into the university career is in this country the exception among the younger instructors. Those exceptions must become the rule before the whole level of production will be raised. As soon as the first-class men are drawn to it, no quantity of work will harm them; men of that stamp have the vitality to do first-class

work under any circumstances. America cannot
bring it about by means of decorations and titles,
and, as in England, baronetcies; and it cannot
start with social prestige, as social prestige is
naturally only a consequence of first-class work
and of the participation of first-class men. High
salaries are, therefore, at present, the only means
which the country has at its disposal.

I well remember a long conversation which I
had with one of the best English scholars, who
came over here to lecture when I had been only
a short time in the country, and was without experience in American academic affairs. We spoke
about the disappointingly low level of American
scholarship, and he said : " America will not have
first-class scholarship, in the sense in which Germany or England has it, till every professor in the
leading universities has at least ten thousand dollars salary, and the best scholars receive twenty-
five thousand dollars." I was distinctly shocked,
and called it a pessimistic and materialistic view.
But he insisted : " No, the American is not anxious
for the money itself ; but money is to him the
measure of success, and therefore the career needs
the backing of money to raise it to social respect
and attractiveness, and to win over the finest
minds." My English acquaintance did not convince me at that time, but the years have con-

vinced me : the years which have brought me into
contact with hundreds of students and instructors
in the whole land ; the years in which I have
watched the development of some of the finest students, who hesitated long whether to follow their
inclination toward scholarship, and who finally
went into law or into business for the sake of the
social premiums.

As soon as the best men are attracted and excellent work is really done, the development will
be a natural one. On the one hand, the community will begin to understand the great meaning
of productive scholarship, and its world-wide difference from receptive and distributing scholarship ; university work will thus get its social recognition, and the ambition to be a productive
scholar — not merely a pleasant author — will be
the highest stimulus in itself, and will secure for
all time the highest standard. Then, also, the
question of salaries will become quite secondary.
America has no difficulty in filling the positions
of ambassadors, even though the expenses are not
seldom three times greater than the salaries. In
the same way, Germany would be able to fill its
professorial chairs if they brought no salary at
all ; the honor of the place rewards its holder,
but at first this honor must be made clear to the
community. On the other hand, as soon as the

really best men go into the work, they must break that too narrow form which is the relic of an unproductive past : teaching in a college cannot be then any longer the necessary preparation for a real university position. Something like the German institution of the docent, which keeps the young scholar from the beginning in the large university, with work according to his own taste, must become the rule. That would bring secondary changes in the administration, which would make the difference between college and university still more marked. The graduate school would become more and more the place for real intellectual independence, and reinforcing in the university teachers the spirit of scholarly production. And this, again, would set higher standards for those college teachers who feel the stimulus to creative scholarship; as candidates for the university professorships, these men would stand in line with the docents, as every vacant chair would be filled by the author of the most important contributions to human knowledge. Thus a mutual stimulation would bring about a new academic situation, in which American scholarship would become equal to the best European production ; but that condition can never be reached as long as the university keeps up artificially the forms and the spirit of the college.

Of course all such considerations lose their power and meaning as soon as the end and purpose is contested. Whoever imagines that productive scholarship is a kind of dreamy idleness, which is of no use for a busy nation, can have no interest in anything which goes beyond a liberal education, and he will be quite willing to import from Europe the material of new thoughts for that liberal education. This is not the place to repeat all the commonplaces which point out the utter absurdity of such a view. I do not care to demonstrate here that even material welfare, industry, and commerce and war, health and wealth, are from year to year increasingly dependent upon the quiet work of scholars and scientists, — work done without direct practical aim, done merely for the honor of truth. And still less do I desire to enter upon sounding declarations that the real civilization of a nation is expressed, not by its material achievements, but by the energies which are working in it toward the moral life and the search for truth and the creation of beauty. I have spoken here only to those who agree that America must not stand behind any nation in its real productive scholarship, in its intellectual creation, in its power to mould the thoughts of the world.

The only sound objection seems the familiar one that Americans have no talent for scholarship.

It has been said that, just as England has no great composer, America will never have a great scholar. I do not believe that. At the middle of the seventeenth century all the nations of Europe had great philosophers, — Bacon and Hobbes in England, Descartes and Malebranche in France, Grotius and Spinoza in Holland, Bruno and Campanella in Italy; and only Germany had the reputation of having no talent for philosophy. It was just before Leibnitz appeared on the horizon, and Kant and Fichte and Hegel followed, and Germany became the centre of philosophy. As soon as the right conditions are given, here too new energies will rush to the foreground. In carefully watching, year after year, American students, I am fully convinced that their talent for productive scholarship is certainly not less than that of the best German students. Compared with them, our students have an inferior training in hard systematic work, as their secondary school education is usually inferior; but I do not wish to touch again upon that dangerous chapter. And secondly, they have infinitely poorer chances for scholarly work in their future, as I have fully pointed out. With a more strenuous preparatory training behind them, and a more favorable opportunity for productive work before them, these students would be the noblest material from which to develop American scholarship.

And I gain my strongest conviction and belief in American scholarship from my admiration for all that the scholars of the past and of the present have done. Indeed, it is with enthusiasm that I look upon the personal achievements in scholarship all over the land. Not only in Harvard, where I see the memory of noble scholars like Agassiz and Peirce, Gray and Child, honored and imitated, and where in my own philosophical department colleagues of eminent creative power set the standard; no, in the most different universities, and often even in small colleges, I have admired the productiveness of brilliant scholars. Yet I have always felt instinctively how much more of lasting value these scores of scholars might have produced, had not all the social factors, all the external conditions, all the public institutions and public moods, worked against them, and hindered and hampered their splendid work. Yes, I should not have expressed any of these considerations did I not hope that it will be clear to every one that all my criticism is directed merely against the system, and never against persons. American scholarship as a whole is so far weak, and not to be compared with America's achievements in technique and industry, in commerce and public education; inferior even to its poetry and architecture. But it is merely because the institutions are undeveloped; the best musicians cannot play a symphony on a fiddle and a drum. Yet it is wonderful how much has been done in the last twenty years against and in spite of the public spirit; how much, after all, has been produced while everything was crushing the zeal for production. This fact, that America has accomplished something, even under the most adverse circumstances, strongly inspires the hope that it will do great things when once the circumstances shall be as favorable as they are in Germany; that is, when the university work is by its aims clearly separated from the work of the lower college classes, when the calls to university chairs are made first of all with reference to scholarly production, when the young scholar has a chance to remain as docent from the beginning in advanced university work, and when the social side of the profession is so developed that it attracts the best men of the country. The development of the institutions, on the other hand, has been such a rapid one in the last years that certainly the hope is justified that the last step will soon be taken: the time is ripe for it. Then the universities will become the soul of the country, and productive scholarship will be the soul of the universities; the best men will then enter into their service, and the productive scholarship of the country will be gigantic in just proportion to its resources.

IV

WOMEN

I

Not long ago, I had an enjoyable call from a young German whose purpose in crossing the ocean was to catch a glimpse of American life. Very naturally we talked, as fellow countrymen do, of the impressions which the New World makes upon the foreigner who has just reached its shores. I asked him whether he kept a diary. He declared that he did not have time for that; but he showed me a little pocket registry in which he was accustomed, as a man of business, to enter his debits, credits, and doubtful accounts. Further on in it, he had instituted a similar reckoning with America. He explained that this was the briefest way of grouping his impressions. I have forgotten the most of these, since the record was one of considerable length; but of the credits I remember distinctly such items as the parlor cars, oysters, waterfalls, shoes, autumn leaves, libraries, after-dinner speeches, the city of Boston, the ice-cream, the hospitality, the " Atlantic

Monthly," etc. Then came the doubtful accounts: the newspapers, mince pies, millionaires, sleeping cars, furnaces, negroes, receptions, poets, the city of New York, etc., etc. And finally came the debits: monuments, politicians, boarding houses, the spring weather, servants, street cleaning, committee meetings, pavements, sauces, and at least three pages more. But what impressed me most of all — and by reason of which the little book comes to my mind at this moment — was a simple "family division" that I found there: under the debits the children, under the doubtful accounts the men, and under the credits the women.

It gave in so simple a formula what all of us had felt during our first months in the New World! We were all amazed at the pert and disrespectful children, and we were all fascinated by the American women. Now and then arose in our souls, perhaps, a slight suspicion as to whether these two things can really go together: it seems so much more natural to expect that a perfect woman will provide also for a perfect education of her children; but whenever we met this woman herself, whenever we saw her and heard her, all skepticism faded away; she was the perfection of Eve's sex. And one group always attracts our attention the most keenly, — the college bred woman. There are beautiful and brilliant and

clever and energetic women the world over, but
the college girl is a new type to us, and, next to
the twenty-four story buildings, nothing excites
our curiosity more than the women who have
their bachelor's degree. Some mingle with their
curiosity certain objections on principle. They
remember that the woman has some grains less of
brain substance than the man, and that every
woman who has learned Greek is considered a
grotesque bluestocking. But even he who is
most violently prejudiced is first reconciled, and
then becomes enthusiastic in theory or married in
practice. He wanders in vain through the colleges to find the repulsive creature he expected,
and the funny picture of the German comic
papers changes slowly into an enchanting type
by Gibson. And when he has made good use of
his letters of introduction, and has met these new
creations at closer range, has chatted with them
before cosy open fires, has danced and bicycled
and golfed with them, has seen their clubs and
meetings and charities, — he finds himself dis-
couragingly word-poor when he endeavors to
describe, with his imperfect English, the impression that has been made upon him ; he feels that
his vocabulary is not sufficiently provided with
complimentary epithets. The American woman
is clever and ingenious and witty ; she is brilliant

and lively and strong; she is charming and beautiful and noble; she is generous and amiable and resolute; she is energetic and practical, and yet idealistic and enthusiastic — indeed, what is she not?

And when we are in our own country once more, we of course play the reformer, and join heartily the ranks of those who fight for the rights of women and for their higher education. I have myself stood in that line. Some years ago, — after my first visit to America, the problem of women and the universities was much discussed in Germany, and about one hundred university professors were asked for their opinions, which were published in a volume entitled " The Academic Woman." And when I sat down to furnish my own contribution to this subject, there appeared before my grateful imagination the lovely pictures of the college yards which I had seen from New England to California; I saw once more the sedate library halls where the fair girls in light-colored gowns radiated joy and happiness; I saw before me the Ivy procession of the Smith College students; I saw again the most charming theatrical performance I have ever enjoyed, the Midsummer Night's Dream, given by Wellesley students on a spring day in the woods by the lake; I saw once more

the eager students in cap and gown in front of
Pembroke Hall, at Bryn Mawr, and I saw once
more the Radcliffe Philosophy Club, where we
prolonged our discussions through so many delightful evenings. A German Wellesley and
Bryn Mawr, I exclaimed, a German Smith and
Vassar, — that is the pressing need of our fatherland! My enthusiastic article was reprinted and
quoted in the discussions, up and down the land;
thus I found myself suddenly marching in line
with the friends of woman's emancipation; and
I was proud that I — the first one in my German
university to do so — had admitted women as
regular students into my laboratory, years before
I came to America.

All that was long ago. I do not now see
American life with the eyes of a newcomer.
That does not mean that I to-day admire American women less than before, nor does it mean
that I falter in my hopes that Germany will absorb American ideas in the realm of higher education for girls. All these feelings remain the
same, and yet, since the surface view of the tourist has been replaced by insight into the deeper
mechanism, my creed has changed. I believe to-
day that it is no less important for America to be
influenced by the German ideals of a woman's
life than for Germany to learn from America.

Of course when I speak of German ideals, I do not mean that witless parody which decorates the speeches of woman suffragists. I mean the real German woman, who is to Americans who have a chance to come into full contact with German life mostly something of a surprise. They expected a slave or a doll, a narrow-minded creature without intelligence and interests, and now their experience is like that of a lady from Boston, — if I may be allowed to make use of her home letter, — who finds that every woman with whom she becomes acquainted in Germany has her serious special interests ; that they are all quite other than she had imagined them. And what is much to the point, the Germany of to-day is not that of twenty years ago. The immense industrial development of the whole country, which has brought wealth and strength and fullness of life into the whole organism, and which has raised the standard of social existence, has left no sphere of German life untouched.

The efforts of this new Germany in the interests of the woman have taken four different forms, — four tendencies which naturally hang together, but externally are sometimes even antagonistic. The first movement, which applies to the largest number of individuals, is that which tends to soften the hardships of the female wage-

earner, especially among the laborers. The second seeks to raise the character of the general
education of girls in the higher classes. The
third endeavors to open new sources of income
to the better educated women of narrow circumstances, and the fourth has as its aim the clearing
of the way for women of special talent, that they
may live out their genius for the good of human-
ity. I have said that these impulses move partly
in opposite directions ; to widen the horizon of
the women of the higher classes and to prepare
them for professional work means to draw them
away from the hearth, while all the efforts in be-
half of the women in the mills and shops tend to
bring them again to the hearth of the home.
The one group gave too much time to the mere
household, in its narrowest sense ; the other group
had too little time for this. The progress in all
four directions is almost a rapid one ; the legislation in the interest, and for the protection, of
working-women is a model for the world ; and —
to point to the top of the pyramid — the conservative universities have opened wide their doors.
Last winter 431 women were admitted to the
University of Berlin alone.

These four tendencies, which ought to remain
clearly separated in every discussion, as the usual
mixing of them brings confusion, have neverthe-

less a single background of principles. One of
these, which sounds of course utterly commonplace, is, that it must remain the central function
of the woman to be wife and mother; and the
other is that public life and culture, including
politics, public morality, science, art, higher education, industry, commerce, law, literature, the
newspaper, and the church, are produced, formed,
and stamped by men. I do not mean that every
woman, or even every man who works for woman's rights in Germany to-day is ready to acknowledge these two principles. The social-democratic party, whose spokesman, Bebel, has written
a most striking book on the woman, would reject
these principles decidedly; and whoever plunges
into the literature of the more radical wing must
hear at once that free love is the only decent rule,
and that every blunder in civilization has come
from the old-fashioned notion that men may med-
dle with public affairs instead of trusting them
to the judgment of women. But all these de-
clamations have accomplished nothing; they have
not removed a single pebble from the path of the
woman. Every tendency that strikes against
those two fundamental principles of German conviction has been paralyzed by the spirit of the
country. It may be said, without exaggeration,
that all the efforts towards the solution of the

woman question in Germany strengthen and reinforce the family idea. The only exceptions to
this are the liberal provisions for the highest
development of women of unusual talent; but
genius must always be treated as an exception,
and such exceptions have existed at all times.
The few who take the doctor's degree, and who
feel the mission for productive work in scholarship, can thus be set aside in the discussion, while
the situation as a whole suggests most clearly the
irregularity of such a vocation, and does not push
the average woman into such a path.

The three remaining movements alone have a
typical value. But there cannot be the slightest
doubt that all that tends to uplift the lot of the
working-woman protects first the home as a whole
in protecting the individual girl or wife or mother.
The central endeavor is to give her time for the
household cares, and for her functions as a member of the family. The higher education, on the
other hand, in so far as it does not aim at the
exceptional achievements of the highest scholarship, is almost wholly in Germany of a character
to make the young women better fitted for marriage. That the average girl attains to the
fulfillment of her hopes only in marriage is a
practical dogma which finds in the wide masses
there no doubters; and that, in the better classes,

the education of the woman was for a long time so
much inferior to that of the man that it seriously
interfered with a deeper intellectual comradeship
in married life, also cannot be denied.   The successful efforts to raise the standard of female
education, and to bring it nearer to the level of
that of young men, has thus the tendency to give
new attractiveness to the family life, and to make
the girl more marriageable. In the atmosphere of
the present German social views, — others may call
them prejudices, — these efforts do not contain
the least factor that operates against the crystal-
lization of households.   The more the horizon of
the man widens with the new wealth and expansion of the modern Germany, the more this ena-
bles the girl, in the struggle for married existence,
to bring into the home a richer intellectual life,
for which the need was less felt in the more idyllic
and provincial German homes of the past generation.   Finally, the increased opportunities for
German women to earn their own living make not
at all in the Fatherland against the establishment
of the home. These opportunities lift, indeed,
from many homes the burdens of misery, and
make many empty and wasted lives useful ; but,
under the existing conditions of public opinion,
there is no fear that they will ever have any
chances as substitutes for marriage.   They re-

main, for the large masses, necessarily the second best choice; a question, on the whole, merely for those who have had no chance to marry, or who are afraid that they will not marry, or who hope that it will somehow help them to marry. In Germany, where the female sex outnumbers the male in such a high degree, and where, besides, about ten per cent of the men prefer to stay in their bachelor quarters, a million women have to seek other spheres than that of the wife; but no average German girl desires to be one of that million, even did the new opportunities that are constantly opening up offer a little better salary than is the case to-day. And, finally, does any one who has obtained even a glimpse of German civilization need any further proof that the whole public culture there is stamped by man's mind? No reasonable German considers the function of woman in the social organism less important or less noble than that of man, but the public questions he wishes to have settled by men. Man sets the standard in every public discussion, for politics and civil life, for science and scholarship, for education and religion, for law and medicine, for commerce and industry, and even for art and literature. Women are faithful helpers there in some lines, — they assist and disseminate, and in art and literature their work may reach the highest level;

but the landmarks for every development are set by men, and all this will outlast even the most energetic movements for the higher education of woman, unless the whole structure of German ideals becomes disorganized.

II

In both respects, in relation to the home and in relation to the standards of public culture, the movements in the interest of women have in America exactly the opposite tendency from those in Germany; even the same facts have, under the different social conditions, an absolutely different meaning : the whole situation here militates against the home and against the masculine control of higher culture, and seems to me, therefore, antagonistic to the health of the nation. I shall consider first the influence on the home. I am not so unfair as to deduce my conclusions from the radical speeches of ill-balanced reformers, or from the experimental extravagances of social iconoclasts; I do not speak of those who want to see the children brought up in government institutions from the first days of life, or of those who consider marriage as the only surviving slavery. No; I do not think of dreams and revolutions; I have the actual, present situation in mind, the facts as they are welcomed by the conservative population.

And yet, with this alone in mind, I feel convinced that serious forces are at work to undermine the home, and to antagonize the formation of families.

Of course I will not warm up the old-fashioned argument, which is repeated so often in Europe, that the higher learning makes a girl awkward and ill-mannered, and that the man will never be drawn to such a bluestocking: I take for granted that no American girl loses in attractiveness by passing through a college, or through other forms of the higher and the highest education. But we have only to look at the case from the other side, and we shall find ourselves at once at the true source of the calamity. The woman has not become less attractive as regards marriage; but has not marriage become less attractive to the woman? and long before the freshman year did not the outer influences begin to impel in that direction? does it not begin in every country school where the girls sit on the same bench with the boys, and discover, a long, long time too early, how stupid those boys are? Coeducation, on the whole unknown in Germany, has many desirable features, — it strengthens the girls; it refines the boys; it creates a comradeship between the two sexes which decreases sexual tension in the years of development; but these factors make, at the same time, for an indifference

toward the other sex, toward a disillusionism,
which must show in the end. The average German girl thinks, I am sorry to say, that she will
marry any one who will not make her unhappy ;
the ideal German girl thinks that she will marry
only the man who will certainly make her happy;
the ideal American girl thinks that she can marry
only the man without whom she will be unhappy;
and the average American girl approaches this
standpoint with an alarming rapidity. Now, is
not the last a much more ideal point of view?
does it not indicate a much nobler type of woman,
— the one who will have no marriage but the
most ideal one, as compared with the other, who
in a romantic desire for marriage takes the first
man who asks her ? But in this connection, I
do not wish to approve or to criticise; we may post-
pone that until we have gathered a few more facts
and motives. Coeducation is only one ; a whole
corona of motives surrounds it.

Coeducation means only equality ; but the so-
called higher education for girls means, under
the conditions of the American life of to-day, decidedly not the equality, but the superiority of
women. In Germany, even the best educated
woman — with the exception once more of the
few rare and ambitious scholars — feels her education inferior to that of the young man of the

same set, and thus inferior to the mental training of her probable husband. The foundations of his knowledge lie deeper, and the whole structure is built up in a more systematic way. This is true of every one who has passed through a gymnasium, and how much more is it true of those who have gone through the university! Law, medicine, divinity, engineering, and the academic studies of the prospective teacher are in Germany all based essentially upon a scholarly training, and are thus, first of all, factors of general education, — powers to widen the horizon of the intellect. All this is less true in America: the lawyer, the physician, the teacher, the engineer, obtain excellent preparation for the profession: but in a lower degree his studies continue his general culture and education; and the elective system allows him to anticipate the professional training even in college. And, on the other side, as for the business man who may have gone through college with a general education in view — how much, or, better, how little of his culture can be kept alive? Commerce and industry, finance and politics absorb him, and the beautiful college time becomes a dream; the intellectual energies, the factors of general culture, become rusty from disuse; while she, the fortunate college girl, remains in that atmosphere of mental

interests and inspiration, where the power she has
gained remains fresh through contact with books.
The men read newspapers, and, after a while,
just when the time for marriage approaches, she
is his superior, through and through, in intellectual refinement and spiritual standards. And all
this we claim in the case of the man who has had
a college education; but the probability is very
great that he has not had even that. The result
is a marriage in which the woman looks down
upon the culture of her husband; and, as the girl
instinctively feels that it is torture to be the wife
of a man whom she does not respect, she hesi-
tates, and waits, and shrinks before the thought
of entering upon a union that has so few charms.

And can we overlook another side of the delightful college time? No noise of the bustling
world disturbed the peace of the college campus;
no social distinctions influenced the ideal balance
of moral and intellectual and æsthetic energies:
it was an artificial world in which our young
friends lived during the most beautiful years of
their lives. Can we be surprised that they instinctively desire to live on in this peculiar setting
of the stage, with all its Bengal lights and its
self-centred interests? They feel almost uncon-
sciously that all this changes when they marry,
when they are mistresses of a household, — a sit-

uation which, perhaps, means narrowness and
social limitation. They feel that it would be like
an awakening from a lofty dream. There is no
need to awake ; the life in the artificial setting of
remote ideals can be continued, if they attach
themselves, not to a husband and children, but to
clubs and committees, to higher institutions and
charity work, to art and literature ; if they remain thus in a world where everything is so much
more ideal than in that ungainly one in which
children may have the whooping-cough.

Of course all these are not motives that pro-
hibit marriage ; they may not even, in any individual case, work as conscious considerations ; they
are only subconscious energies, which show their
effects merely if you consider the large groups ;
they are the little forces, the accumulation of
which pushes the balance of motives perhaps so
little that they remain unnoticed by the girl who
is undecided whether to accept him; and yet they
are efficient.

The college studies do not merely widen the
horizon ; they give to many a student a concrete
scholarly interest, and that is, of course, still truer
of the professional training. The woman who
studies medicine or natural science, music or
painting, perhaps even law or divinity, can we
affront her with the suggestion, which would be

an insult to the man, that all her work is so superficial that she will not care for its continuation
as soon as she undertakes the duties of a married
woman? Or ought we to imply that she is so
conceited as to believe that she is able to do what
no man would dare hope for himself; that is, to
combine the professional duties of the man with
the not less complex duties of the woman? She
knows that the intensity of her special interest
must suffer; that her work must become a superficial side-interest; that she has for it but rare
leisure hours; and no one can blame her, however much she may love her own home, for loving
still more the fascinating work for which she was
trained.

All these tendencies are now psychologically
reinforced by other factors which have nothing
to do with the higher education as such, but are
characteristic of the situation of the woman in
general. The American girl, well or carelessly
educated, lives in the midst of social enjoyments,
of cultured interests, of flirtations, and of refine-
ments — what has she to hope at all from the
change which marriage brings? Well, the one
without whom her heart would break may have
appeared — there is then no use of further discussion. But it is more probable that he has not
appeared, while she, in the meanwhile, flirts with

half a dozen men, of whom one is so congenial, and another such a brilliant wit, and the third such a promising and clever fellow; the fourth is rich, and the fifth she has known since her childhood, and the sixth, with the best chances, is such a dear, stupid little thing! What has she really to gain from a revolution of her individual fate? Is there anything open to her which was closed so far? Between the social freedom of a German girl and a German wife there is not that gulf which separates the two groups, for instance, in France; and yet the change from the single to the married life is an absolute one. Even in Germany, the joys of girlhood have something of the provisional in their character, like the temporary filling of a time of preparation for the real life. In this country the opposite prevails. Every foreigner sees with amazement the social liberty of the young girl, and admires no great American invention more than the unique system of the chaperon. He is thus hardly surprised that the American girl almost hides the fact when she becomes engaged; she has to give up so many fine things, — a period almost of resignation has to begin, and no new, untried social enjoyments are in view.

III

But the American girl has not only no new powers to expect; she has in marriage a positive function before her, which she, again unlike her European sister, considers, on the whole, a burden, — the care of the household. I do not mean that the German woman is enraptured with delight at the prospect of scrubbing a floor ; and I know, of course, how many American women are model housekeepers, how the farmers' wives, especially, have their pride in it, and how often spoiled girls heroically undertake housekeeping with narrow means, and that, too, much more often than in Germany, without the help of servants. And yet, there remains a difference of general attitude which the social psychologist cannot overlook. The whole atmosphere is here filled with the conscious or unconscious theory that housework is somewhat commonplace, a sort of necessary evil which ought to be reduced to a minimum. I do not ask whether that is not perhaps correct; I insist only that this feeling is much stronger here than in Germany, and that it must thus work against domestic life. I point merely to a few symptoms of this phenomenon. I think, for instance, of the boarding-house life of married people, an anti-domestic custom which has such wide

extension in America, and which is not only unknown, but utterly inconceivable in Germany.
But also where a house is kept, the outsider has
the feeling that the young wife enjoys her home
as the basis of family life and as a social background, but that she is not trained to enjoy it
as a field of domestic activity. The German
girl anticipates, not as the smallest enjoyment of
marriage, the possession of a household after her
own domestic tastes, and according to her talent
for housework. Her whole home education is a
preparation for this, and here the German mother finds a large share of her duties. All this
may be, in a way, an unpractical scheme; it may
be wasted energy; it may be better to learn those
functions in a more mature age, in which the
mind approaches them more theoretically; but
this at least is certain, that the German way develops a more instinctive inclination toward the
home life.

The general American tendency to consider
housework as a kind of necessary evil, which as
such cannot appeal to those who have free choice,
is not less evident in the lower strata of the community. The conviction of every American girl
that it is dignified to work in the mill, but undignified to be a cook in any other family, would
never have reached its present intensity if an

anti-domestic feeling were not in the background.
Exactly the same tendency appears, therefore,
when work for the parents is in question. The
laborer's daughter has, of course, not such a complete theory as the banker's daughter; but that
it is dull to sit in the kitchen and look after the
little sister, she too knows. In consequence, she
also rushes to the outside life as saleswoman, as
industrial laborer, as office worker : it is so exciting and interesting ; it is the richer life. The
study of the special cases shows, of course, that
there are innumerable factors involved ; but if
we seek for the most striking features of woman's
work, here and abroad, from a more general sur-
vey of the subject, it would seem that the aim of
the German woman is to further the interests of
the household, and that of the American woman
to escape from the household.

Germany, with its very condensed population,
was not able to do without the help of female
muscle in running the economic machine ; America, with its thin population and its great natural
richness, does not really need this. In Germany
almost a fourth of the women are at work; in
America hardly more than a tenth. Above all,
in Germany the women are doing the hard work,
two and a half millions being engaged in agricul-
ture against half a million here, of whom the

greater part are negroes. The condition of the
country as a whole does not demand woman's
aid; man's labor can support the households of
this country, and, economically, the country
would be better off if female labor were almost
entirely suppressed, both by prejudice and by institutions, since it lowers the wages of the men,
and wastes domestic energies which, in a more
intensified effort, would save the more. If, in
spite of these economic conditions, woman's labor,
other than of a domestic character, has become a
socially necessary factor, it must have been, first
of all, because the American woman feels that it
is easier to perform the labor of the man than to
make an increased domestic effort. It is the dis-
inclination to domestic cares that has slowly
created the present situation, and this situation,
itself, with its resulting distribution of wages, has
necessarily the effect of reinforcing this motive,
and of pushing the woman from the hearth to
the mill and the salesroom, the office and the
classroom.

I have mentioned merely mental factors which
are to be taken into account in their subconscious
coöperation against family life; but the mental
strain and excitement to which young girls are
subjected, and the lack of social restraint, the
constant hurry, and, above all, the intellectual

over-tension must influence the nervous system, and the nervous system must influence the whole organization of that sex which nature, after all, has made the weaker one. The foreigner cannot see these charming American girls without a constant feeling that there is something unhealthy in their nervous make-up, an over-irritation, a pathological tension, not desirable for the woman who is preparing herself to be the mother of healthy children. The vital statistics tell the whole story. The census of 1890 showed that there were born per thousand of the whole population in Prussia 36.6, in Massachusetts 21.5; and this diminished birth rate is still much lower in the native families here than in those of foreign birth, — the Irish or Swedish or German.

If we will consider this social background, this general social situation, we shall perhaps see the problem of higher education from another point of view; we shall begin to feel that under these conditions, which in themselves work so clearly against the home, it must be doubly dangerous to reinforce those tendencies in woman's higher education which, as such, impel toward a celibacy of spirit; and we foreigners ask ourselves then instinctively, " Is the woman question really solved here in the most ideal way ? "

The answer which every one of my American

friends, male and female, has ready on his lips is very simple. Can you deny, they ask, that the woman whom you accuse is a higher type of human being than any other? Do you want her to be untrue to her ideals, to seek marriage just for marriage's sake, instead of waiting for the man of her higher hopes? But such answers do not help me at all. It may be that I am willing to concede that place of honor to the individual girl here, in comparison with the girl of other nations, but the real problem cannot be even approached as long as the individual is in question. Here lies the point where, according to German convictions, the shortcomings of American civilization arise: to the American mind the community is a multitude of individuals, to the German mind it is above all a unity. The American sees in the state an accumulation of elements of which each ought to be as perfect as possible; the German sees in it an organism in which each element ideally fulfills its rôle, only in so far as it adjusts itself to the welfare and perfection of the whole. It is the atomistic idea of the community as against the organic one; the naturalistic aspect as against the historical; the state as a sandhill where every grain is independent of every other, against the state as a living being where every cell is in internal connection with every other.

If it were really the goal of civilization to inspire the individuals that are now alive with as high aims as possible, the American system would be, at least with regard to the women, an ideal one; but if, to mention at first this single point, such a system works against the creation of substitutes for the individuals who have outlived their life, and thus destroys in the nation the power of rejuvenation, it is clear that the goal was wrongly chosen, and that the standard of perfection cannot be made dependent merely upon personal achievement.

Indeed, not the slightest reproach attaches to the individual girl who does not wish to marry because her education and her social surroundings have given her ideals which she can fulfill only in celibacy; she stands individually much higher than the other, who with the same views of life nevertheless marries, and perhaps becomes untrue to her ideals, sacrificing her lofty scholarly ambitions for mere idle comfort. But the reproach must be directed against the community which gives to the girls an education and an inspiration which lead to such a conflict, and thus antagonize the natural energies of a healthy nation. Such a system is made according to an artificial ideal; there is in the world of experience no individual which rests and reposes in or on itself: the natural unity is the family. Every system of public spirit which in its final outcome raises the individuals, but lowers the families, is antagonistic to the true civilization of the people, and its individualistic, brilliant achievements are dearly bought illusions of success. No one will dare say to a woman, This is the best, but you, for one, ought to be satisfied with the second best. But we have the right to demand from the community that the woman be taught to consider, as the really best for her, what is in the highest interests of the whole of society, even if it be second best for the individual.

What can be done? Is it necessary to lower the standard of woman's education in all levels of society in order to reinforce the family feeling? Must we throw away all that is achieved for the self-preservation of the race? or is there possibly a way to maintain this glorious individual perfection, and yet to serve the purposes of the organic community? But the answer to this practical question may be postponed until we have considered, more briefly, the other factor to which I have already referred. I affirmed that in Germany all the movements in the field of the woman question are not only in harmony with, and in the interest of, the family, but that, above all, the whole public life bears, as a matter of course, the stamp of the man. That is, in my opinion, the second great difference. The American system injures the national organism, not only because it antagonizes the family life, and thus diminishes the chances for the future bearers of the national civilization, but it has, secondly, the tendency to feminize the whole higher culture, and thus to injure the national civilization itself.

IV

If I speak of public life here, I do not mean politics in the technical sense. The arguments for and against the participation of women in politics, the reasons for and against woman suffrage, are certainly of a peculiar kind; I have often listened to both sides in these discussions, and have always, as long as one side was pleading its cause, felt strongly in favor of the other side. If I am, on the whole, opposed to woman suffrage, it is because it belongs to those factors which we have discussed : it would help to draw the interests of individual women away from domestic life. But I do not think that it would have a serious bearing on that point which we have now to consider, the effemination of public life. Politics would certainly be influenced as to its character if woman suffrage existed everywhere, — it would, in some ways, probably suffer through hysterical sentimentality, illogical impulses, and the lack of consistent obedience to abstract law; but it would probably be, on the other hand, in many respects ennobled and moralized, softened and elevated. There would be, on the whole, no serious disadvantage to be feared for political life itself, because the men would always remain the backbone of the political parties. Politics in America so immediately and directly penetrates man's whole welfare, his commerce and industry, his income and his expenses, his rights and his duty, that there is no danger that he would ever allow the political life to pass from his hands into those of the woman; a real effeminizing of political life is thus no probable danger. Of course, so long as only four of the less developed States of the Union have introduced woman suffrage, the question is of no practical importance.

The public life that I have in mind is the public expression of the ideal energies, the striving for truth and beauty, for morality and religion, for education and social reform, and their embodiment, not in the home, but in the public consciousness. In Germany no one of these functions of public life is without the support and ennobling influence of active women, but decidedly the real bulk of the work is done by men; they alone give to it character and direction, and

their controlling influence gives to this whole
manifoldness of national aims its strenuousness
and unity ; to carry these into the millions of
homes and to make them living factors in the
family, is the great task of the women there.
Here, on the other hand, the women are the real
supporters of the ideal endeavors : in not a few
fields, their influence is the decisive one ; in all
fields, this influence is felt, and the whole system
tends ever more and more to push the men out
and the women in. Theatre managers claim that
eighty-five per cent. of their patrons are women.
No one can doubt that the same percentage would
hold for those who attend art exhibitions, and
even for those who read magazines and literary
works in general. And we might as well continue with the same somewhat arbitrary figure :
can we deny that there are about eighty-five per
cent of women among those who attend public
lectures, or who go to concerts, among those who
look after public charities and the work of the
churches ? I do not remember ever to have been
in a German art exhibition where at least half of
those present were not men, but I do remember
art exhibitions in Boston, New York, and Chicago
where according to my actual count the men in
the hall were less than five per cent of those present. As a matter of course, the patron deter-

mines the direction which the development will take. As the political reader is more responsible for the yellow press than is the editor, so all the non-political functions of public life must slowly take, under these conditions, the stamp of the feminine taste and type, which must have again the further effect of repelling man from it more and more. The result is an effemination of the higher culture, which is antagonistic to the development of a really representative national civilization, and which is not less unsound and onesided than the opposite extreme of certain Oriental nations, where the whole culture is man's work, and the woman a slave in the harem.

The woman, and sometimes even the indolent man who wants to get rid of the responsibility of something he does not care about, says simply that this is all right. As the facts show — they argue — that the woman is not inferior in intellectual and æsthetic energies, not inferior in earnestness and enthusiasm, why not intrust her with the national culture, why not give her full charge of art and literature, education and science, morality and religion — man has a sufficient number of other things to do. But it is simply not true, and cannot be made true by any dialectics, that the minds of man and woman are equal, and can be substituted the one for the other, without changing the entire character of the mental product. It is not true that men and women can do the same work in every line. Earnestness certainly the women have. However large the number of those who may meet their public duties in a spirit of sport or amusement or ennui, the majority take these duties seriously; and the college girl especially comes home with a large amount of earnestness in the cause of reform and of the higher functions of the national life. The only misfortune is that earnestness alone is not physical energy, that good will is not force, that devotion is not power. But her lack of physical power and strength would be less dangerous to the undertaking if her intellectual ability were equal to that of the man. But here the social psychologist can feel no shadow of a doubt that neither coeducation nor the equality of opportunities has done anything to eliminate those characteristic features of the female mind which are well known the world over, and which it is our blessing not to have lost. The laws of nature are stronger than the theories of men.

To express the matter in a psychological formula, on which the observations of all times and all nations have agreed : in the female mind the contents of consciousness have the tendency to fuse into a unity, while they remain separated in the man's mind. Both tendencies have their merits and their defects; but, above all, they are different, and make women superior in some functions, and man superior in some others. The immediate outcome of that feminine mental type is woman's tact and æsthetic feeling, her instinctive insight, her enthusiasm, her sympathy, her natural wisdom and morality; but, on the other side, also, her lack of clearness and logical consistency, her tendency to hasty generalization, her mixing of principles, her undervaluation of the abstract and of the absent, her lack of deliberation, her readiness to follow her feelings and emotions. Even these defects can beautify the private life, can make our social surroundings attractive, and soften and complete the strenuous, earnest, and consistent public activity of the man; but they do not give the power to meet these public duties without man's harder logic. If the whole national civilization should receive the feminine stamp, it would become powerless and without decisive influence on the world's progress.

On the surface, it seems otherwise. Every one thinks at once of some most talented women, whose training in strenuous thought is not inferior to that of men, and every one knows that our female students are as good scholars as the male ones. Those few exceptions I need not to discuss here, — the genius is *sui generis ;* but the case of the female university students does not at all suggest to me a belief in their intellectual equality with men. Certainly the average female student ranks as a pupil equal to the young man, but that does not exclude the fact that her achievements and his are profoundly different; she is more studious, and thus balances certain undeniable shortcomings, and the subjects in which she excels are other than those in which he is most interested. Above all, — and here I touch an important point too much neglected, — the difference between the students appears relatively small here, because the historic development of the American college has brought it about that the whole higher study bears far too much the type of the feminine attitude towards scholarship; and this is the reason why the scholarly outcome has so far been on the whole unsatisfactory. In Germany, the university professors who are opposed to the admission of women to the university take for granted that the women will be industrious and good pupils, but insist that they will lower the standard of the really scholarly work, because they will take, in accordance with the feminine mind, a passive, receptive, uncritical attitude toward knowledge, while the whole importance of German scholarly life lies in

its active criticism, its strength of research and
inquiry. All that the German professors now
fear from the intrusion of women was precisely
the habitual, characteristic weakness of the American college until a decade or two ago. These
colleges were excellent as places for the distribution of knowledge, but undeveloped as places of
research; they were controlled by a passive belief
in intellectual authorities, but little prepared to
advance the knowledge of the world; in short,
they took the receptive, feminine attitude — no
wonder that the women could do as well as the
men. But in recent time the American university strives with vigorous efforts toward the realization of the higher ideal; the test of the question whether the dogmatic mind of the average
woman will prove equal to that of the average
man, in a place controlled by a spirit of critical
research, has simply not been made so far. If I
except the few rare talents, which have been left
out of our discussion, since they do not require
that systems be adjusted to them, I cannot say
that I have gained the impression that the spirit
of research would be safe in the hands of the
woman. But what a calamity for the country
if this great epoch in the life of the universities were ruined by any concessions to the feminine type of thinking! The nearer America ap-

proaches a state of university work that corresponds to the highest achievements of European
universities, the more it develops real universities
beyond the collegiate institutions for receptive
study, the more the equality of the two sexes
must disappear in them, — the more must they
become, like the European institutions, places for
men, where only the exceptional women of special
talent can be welcomed, while the average woman
must attend the woman's college with its receptive
scholarship. If we keep up an artificial equality
through the higher development of the present
day, American intellectual work will be kept
down by the women, and will never become a
world power.

How differently, when compared with that of
men of the same class, the female mind works, we
see daily around us when we turn our eyes from
the educated level down toward the half-educated
multitude. Here we are confronted with the woman who antagonizes serious medicine through
her belief in patent medicines and quackery, the
woman who undermines moral philosophy through
her rushing into spiritualism and every superstition of the day, the woman who injures the progress of thought and reform by running with
hysterical zeal after every new fad and fashion
introduced with a catchy phrase. A lack of re-

spect for really strenuous thought characterizes woman in general. Dilettantism is the key-note. The half-educated man is much more inclined to show an instinctive respect for trained thought, and to abstain from opinions where he is ignorant. But the half-educated woman cannot discriminate between the superficial and the profound, and, without the slightest hesitation, she effuses, like a bit of gossip, her views on Greek art or on Darwinism or on the human soul, between two spoonfuls of ice-cream. Even that is almost refreshing as a softening supplement to the manly work of civilization, but it would be a misfortune if such a spirit were to gain the controlling influence.

That such effemination makes alarming progress is quickly seen if we watch the development of the teacher's profession. I have seldom the honor of agreeing with the pedagogical scholars of this country, but, on this point, it seems to me, we are all of the same opinion: the disappearance of the man from the classroom, not only of the lower schools, but even of the high schools, is distinctly alarming. The primary school is to-day absolutely monopolized by woman teachers, and in the high school they have the overwhelming majority. The reason for this is clear: since the woman does not have to support a family, she can work for a smaller salary, and thus, as in the mills the men tend more and more toward the places for which women are not strong enough, in the schools, too, female competition must, if no halt is called, bring down salaries to a point from which the supporter of the family must retreat. It would be, of course, in both cases better if the earnings were larger, and more men were thus enabled to support families, while in the school-room, as in the mill, the female competitor brings the earnings down to a point where the man is too poor to marry her, — a most regrettable state of affairs. But the economic side is here not so important as the effect on civilization. Even granting, what I am not at all ready to grant, that woman's work, preferred because it is cheaper to the community, is just as good as man's work, can it be without danger that the male youth of this country, up to the eighteenth year, is educated by unmarried women? Is it a point to be discussed at all that "nascent manhood requires for right development manly inspiration, direction, and control"? Where will this end? That very soon no male school-teacher of good quality will survive is certain, but there is no reason to expect that it will stop there. We have already to-day more than sixty per cent of girls among the upper high-school classes, and this disproportion must increase. Must we not expect that in

the same way in which the last thirty years have
handed the teacher's profession over to the women, the next thirty years will put the ministry,
the medical calling, and, finally the bar, also into
her control? To say that this is not to be feared
because it has never happened anywhere before
is no longer an argument, because this development of our schools is also new in the history of
civilization. There was never before a nation
that gave the education of the young into the
hands of the lowest bidder.

V

The comic papers prophesy alarming results for
the man; while the woman teaches and preaches
and argues before the court, he will have to do
the cooking, mending, and nursing at home.
That is absurd. There is enough room for the
development of man in the present direction.
Commerce and industry, politics and war, will furnish no lack of opportunities for the employment
of all his energies; but one thing is certain : he
will be a stranger to the higher culture of the
nation. And this condition, in which the professional callings, the whole influence on the development of the younger generation, all art and
science and morality and religion, come to be
moulded and stamped by women, is precisely the

one which some call equality of the sexes! The truth is evident, here as everywhere, that equality cannot be brought about artificially. To force equality always means merely shifting the inequality from one region to another; and if the primary inequality was the natural one, the artificial substitute must be dangerous if it be more than a temporary condition. Nature cannot act otherwise, because nature cannot tolerate real equality. Equality means in the household of nature a wasted repetition of function; equality, therefore, represents everywhere the lower stage of the development, and has to go over into differentiation of functions. Nature cannot be dodged, and the growth of nations cannot escape natural laws. To say that man and woman must be equal demands a natural correction by bringing in the differentiation of function at some other point: you may decree equality to-day, but nature takes care that we shall have, in consequence, a new kind of inequality to-morrow. The nation has decreed that the differences of sex shall be ignored in education and in the choice of callings, and the outcome is a greater inequality than in any other country, an inequality in which men are turned out of the realms of higher culture.

But as soon as we take the point of view of social philosophy, we understand at once the

deeper meaning of the whole phenomenon and its
probable development. This cry for equality,
with its necessary results in a new form of crass
inequality, then manifests itself as a great scheme
of nature in the interests of the conservation
of the race, in keeping with the special conditions under which the nation has received its
growth. Under the ordinary conditions, the material opening and settling of a country move
parallel with the development of the inner culture, and the man is thus able to meet the requirements of this twofold public task; he gives
his energies to the material and political necessi-
ties so long as the mental and spiritual culture is
low, and in proportion as he is freed from the
rudimentary needs that pertain to the support of
the nation, he turns to the inner culture, that of
education and art, and so on, while the woman,
at every stage, cares for the private life of the family. In America, this normal course was changed,
because the material opening of the country, the
unfolding of its natural resources, coincided with
the possession of a most complex inner culture
brought over from Europe ready-made, not grown
of the soil. Hence a new division of labor had
to be discovered to meet those material exigen-
cies which demanded man's full energy and man's
side-function, the work of the higher culture,

also. This side-function had to be assumed by the woman ; she had to care for the inner culture of the nation, that the arms of the man might be free for the more immediate work, the settling of the continent, the political organization, and the development of the national wealth. This was, under these unusual conditions, the only way of preserving and fostering the high European culture ; if women had not temporarily taken this function from man, it would have been wholly lost in the wear and tear of the commercial and political adolescence of the nation. It was, then, the special mission of the American woman to become the bearer of the higher, inherited culture of the nation by the artificial development of an intellectual superiority over the man.

But if this be true, it is clear that such vicarious functioning must cease as soon as those two peculiar conditions should arise which manifestly exist at the present time. The first of these conditions is that this female superiority should reach a point where it begins to effeminate the higher culture, and where it becomes antagonistic to family life; thus positively injuring the organism of the race. The other condition is that the material establishment of the country should have attained its completion ; the ground mastered, the sources of national wealth sufficiently developed to allow room for man's effort in other directions. No doubt this condition also is fulfilled to-day, — the West is opened; the whole continent is economically subjugated; a net of transportation covers the whole land; wealth abounds in a sufficient number of families, down to the second and third generations, to insure the building up of a leisure class; and the time has come when the American man can take his share, like the European, in the spiritual culture of his country. If the American man will but turn his real energies to the world of spiritual goods, then the two great evils which we have discussed will both be cured by the one remedy, and at one time, while the woman will not in any respect be the loser. If man takes the part that belongs to him in the higher culture, this, instead of being emasculated, will show that perfect blending of human energies in which the strength of the man will be softened by pure womanhood, and, at the same time, the woman, who will feel the greater strength in the man of equal culture, will shrink no longer from marriage, and will feel attracted by that truer companionship in which the real labor is divided, the public function given to the man, the domestic function to the daughter and sister, to the wife and mother. That is the state at which we aim in Germany; much has still to

be done there to give to the average German woman the thorough education of the American;
but that will soon come. In any case, even the
best training of the woman must support in Germany the family idea, and the man will continue
to be the mainstay of the ideal culture. We Germans feel sure that this will not be endangered,
even if we fully imitate the splendid college life
of American girls. Therefore, no one can suggest that woman's education in this country ought
to take any steps backward; all the glorious opportunities must remain open, and only one practical change must come in response to the urgent
needs of our period: the American man must
raise his level of general culture. In short, the
woman's question is in this country, as ultimately
perhaps everywhere, the man's question. Reform
the man, and all the difficulties disappear.

We know that in Paradise, Eve followed the
seducing voice of the serpent, and ate the fruit
from the tree of knowledge, and gave of it unto
Adam. The college-bred Eve has no smaller
longing for the apple of knowledge; but the serpent has become modern, and his advice has
grown more serpent-like than ever: " Eat of the
apple, but give not unto Adam thereof." The
Bible tells us that when they both ate, they were
cast out from Paradise, but saved the race. How-

ever it may be with the modern paradise, the race will be saved only on the condition that Adam receive his share of the fruit. Listen not to the serpent, but divide the apple!

V

AMERICAN DEMOCRACY

I

A GERMAN who has seen the world and tries to make his thinking free from the chance influences of his surroundings may easily ask himself whether it would not be most desirable that all nations should become republican democracies after the American model. If he does not ask the question himself, he is sure to be asked it by an American friend who happens not to agree with the last speech of the German Emperor, and who, therefore, takes for granted that an educated German, outside of the reach of the German state-attorney, will frankly confess that monarchy is a mediæval relic and that democracy alone is life. When one of my friends approached me the other day with such an inquiry, I was in a hurry, and my answer had to be short. I told him, first, that the achievements of democratic America are not the achievements of American democracy; secondly, that democracy in itself has as many bad tendencies as good ones, and is thus not better than aristocracy;

thirdly, that the question whether democracy or
aristocracy is better does not exist to-day ; fourthly,
that Germany daily becomes more democratic,
while America steadily grows aristocratic ; fifthly,
that there is no difference between the two nations
anyway. My friend insisted that my argument
stood on the same level with the oath of the woman
who was accused before the court of breaking a
pot which she had borrowed from her neighbor,
and who swore, first, that the pot was not broken
when she returned it ; secondly, that the pot was
broken when she borrowed it ; and, thirdly, that
she had not borrowed the pot. Well, that may
be ; but my haste alone was to blame, as I could
not explain in the few words I had time for that democracy can cover very different tendencies. Thus
I promised, when I had leisure, to disentangle my
twisted argument, and to illustrate, perhaps even
to establish it. The following remarks are, as far
as possible, a fulfillment of my promise, and they
follow exactly the order of the argument.

I must begin, therefore, with the inquiry
whether the present civilization of America in its
good and glorious features is to be considered as
evidence in favor of democracy as against aristocracy, of republican institutions as against monarchical.

The eulogists and the critics of American democracy, nowadays, often make their enterprise quite easy by praising or attacking it for qualities which certainly belong to democratic America, but which are not characteristic of American democracy. The trouble, of course, begins at the very outset, with the difficulty of defining what democracy really is. Democracy is equality; and yet we are familiar with the argument of those who insist that equality is a foreign and un-American conception, and that American democracy is not equality, but liberty. Democracy is government by those who are governed; but why, then, no woman suffrage in America? Democracy is government by majorities; and yet a thousand people in the State of New York do not count, as voters for the Senate, more than a dozen in Nevada, and even the President may be chosen by a minority. Democracy means universal suffrage, and yet every constitutional monarchy in Europe is based on universal suffrage. Democracy is brotherhood, but those who know Russia assure us that there is no more brotherly people than that of the Czar. A democracy is a republic; and yet we hear that the American colony was already democratic before the Revolution, that England is, after all, to-day a democracy, and that France is pseudo-democratic only.

It is easy to praise democracy in America if it

is contrasted merely with the demoralized aristocracy of the Louis Quatorze period. The only defect of the argument is that such an aristocracy does not exist anywhere to-day, and that every word of the eulogy thus fits, just as well, any other non-republican country. And it is easy to depreciate American democracy if it be compared with an ideal construction of public life, which is nowhere realized under the most complex conditions of modern society. The criticism, again, can be turned against any other country where, under different forms, the defects of modern culture and the weaknesses of human character bring about similar evils. It happens easily that the American puts into the ledger of democracy too many items which simply belong to the times in which we live.

The unfairness of such a substitution is felt most strongly when America is compared with Germany. Germany has become in the literature of democracy the most convenient object of demonstration for the difference between the New and the Old World system. Comparison with England leads too quickly to the sentiment that the monarchy is there merely decorative; comparison with France is dangerous, since France pretends to be a democracy like America; comparison with Russia is out of the question, partly because Russian life is so little known in America, and partly because its political institutions seem to an American beneath discussion. Germany remains thus in the vast literature of the subject always the one easiest to point to among the leading nations. The popular argument runs as follows: America has all these fine things; America is a democracy; Germany is not a democracy; poor Germany, that cannot have all these fine things! But Germany might very well have them, because they do not necessarily pertain to a democracy as such. It is thus, perhaps, natural to begin a study of American democracy by a comparison of the achievements usually claimed for this country with those of the German Empire, which, as Mr. Bradford in his recent large work on "The Lesson of Popular Government," assures us, "is almost as much under military and imperial despotism as three centuries ago."

It might be difficult to reach a general agreement on any proposed list of reasons for the pride and satisfaction and happiness that result from the public life of this wonderful country, but I have certainly nowhere found in the literature of the subject a more complete enumeration than in the noble essays of Charles W. Eliot, in his recent volume, "American Contributions to Civilization." If I understand him correctly, President Eliot distinguishes ten different features in our public life, each one of which deserves the respect and the admiration of the world. Let us consider these features one by one, as compared with conditions in Germany.. "The first and principal contribution," says President Eliot, " is the advance made in the United States, not in theory only, but in practice, toward the abandonment of war as a means of settling disputes between nations, the substitution of discussion and arbitration, and the avoidance of armaments." That was written in 1896. But it is to the credit of England and not to that of America that the Venezuela conflict did not lead to war in that same year. And since those days we have gone to Cuba, we have gone to the Philippines, and, worse than all, we have heard through the whole scale, from the editorials of the yellow press to the orations of leading senators, the voice of that aggressive temper which waits for an opportunity to show American superiority to the world by battles and not by arbitration. Germany, on the other hand, has now kept the peace for thirty years, peace in a time which was filled to overflowing with international irritations, peace which was paid for with immense expenditures, a peace that almost no one dared to hope for, and which was certainly not a product of chance, but the result of most persistent efforts — it may be added in the same breath, efforts on the part of the government much more than on the part of the people, since in all Europe times have so fully changed that princes are much more peaceably inclined than nations.

"The second eminent contribution which the United States," according to President Eliot, "have made to civilization is their thorough acceptance, in theory and in practice, of the widest religious toleration." "The constitutional prohibition of religious tests as qualifications for office has given the United States the leadership among the nations in dissociating theological opinions and political rights." But again we must ask, is it otherwise in Germany? What office in Germany is dependent upon a religious test? Just as the Protestant population of Saxony loves its Catholic king, and just as the Catholic population of Southern Baden adores the Protestant Grand Duke, so the whole public and political life of Germany shows a peaceable intermingling of all creeds, exactly as in America. If the Americans, to emphasize the contrast with Europe, point to the religious persecutions of the Jews in Russia, we have to consider this as an evidence of race antagonism; and mob violence against other races is certainly not unknown in large parts of America.

On the other hand, the struggle between the German government and the ultramontane Centrist party ought never to be misconstrued as religious intolerance; it is a strictly political fight for power. But religious toleration has not only the political aspect, in which all the leading nations are to-day on the same footing, but also a social aspect; and it may be doubted whether Germany is not superior to America in its willingness to accept the social personality without any intermeddling into the particular way of arranging private relations to the problems of eternity. There is endlessly more personal gossiping about our neighbor's religion here than in Germany. In smaller towns, especially, the social intolerance in religious matters reaches a degree utterly unknown in continental Europe. The American Sunday laws would appear to Germans as an intolerable lack of religious freedom. There is no doubt that even an avowed atheist would find his path much freer in Germany than here.

A third characteristic feature, as is claimed, of American civilization has been the successful development of a manhood suffrage. But every one knows that the legislative bodies of Germany are products of universal suffrage, too, and that the local administration is a highly developed self-government. In both countries universal suffrage

is the great school of political education, the
great vehicle for the feeling of responsibility in
the masses, the means of disseminating public
interests ; but in both countries it needs a complex artificial organization, to be practically man-
ageable, and above all it needs constitutional
limitations to avoid the evident dangers and evils.
All the differences have to do merely with these
forms of adjustment and means of warding
off the dangers. The German system insures,
through the instrumentality of the hereditary
monarchy, those advantages which the founders
of the American Republic secured through the
many conservative features of the American form
of government, where especially the Senate, perhaps not as it is, but as it was planned, and the
prescribed slowness of the governmental proced-
ures, act as an effective restraint upon popular
excitements. If democracy be understood as a
form of government which represents the will
and energies of the people, the German and the
American systems are equally democratic, and it is
wrong to make light of German suffrage because
the highest executive, as representative of the
national will, is not selected by a majority vote,
but by the universal, spontaneous loyalty to one
who stands above parties. On the other hand, it
is not less unfair when English authors are pleased

to call the constitutional the true democracy, and
the American system a pseudo-democracy only.
But so much may be said, indeed, — that the German citizen, when he goes to the ballot-box, receives the educational influences of universal suffrage more directly than his American colleague.
There is no machine, there is no " boss," there is
no two-party system, which often makes the choice
merely a somewhat demoralizing decision between
two evils, or demands a vote on issues which make
no appeal to the personal interests or intelligence
of the voter. The large number of parties in
Germany, on the contrary, lends to the decision a
much more individual character.

A fourth point, which is an occasion of pride to
every American, is " that property has never been
safer under any form of government." But has
any one ever owned a pfennig in Germany behind
which the majesty of the German nation did not
stand ? Certainly it is not otherwise here, but it
cannot be denied that Americans themselves
everywhere reinforce the widespread notion that
the financially weak man cannot find justice in
America against the powerful influences of rich
corporations, a prejudice which has taken much
stronger form in Europe, and has there spread
abroad the erroneous opinion that the American
civil court is a seat of corruption. How much

depends in such questions upon the point of view
is shown by the interesting experience of a large
association founded in New York by German-
Americans. This association gives legal aid to
immigrants, and has in this way been widely beneficial, but when the society recently celebrated
an anniversary, the discussions showed that there
was some difference of opinion as to what they
were really accomplishing. One party believed
that their purpose was to aid the immigrant, who,
by reason of his training in Europe, has not yet
risen to the height of the American doctrine of
equal rights for all; and the other party, on the
contrary, believed that they were to help the immigrant in obtaining justice, because one who is
accustomed to its administration in European
courts will not know how to obtain the " pull "
that is necessary in the unreliable courts of his
new home. If we free ourselves from arbitrary
interpretations of facts and look at the principles,
we shall be sure of the safety of property on both
sides of the ocean.

Is it not a parallel case with the fifth assertion,
" that nowhere have the power and disposition to
read been so general " ? The schooling of the
nation has been for a hundred years the greatest
honor of the fatherland, and, while the completely
illiterate have disappeared in Prussia, it is well

known how large a percentage of native born
whites in the United States are illiterate still, in
how many country districts education is alarmingly crippled, and how often in city schools the
accommodation is insufficient.   On the surface,
the case looks better for the sixth point, "that
nowhere have property and well-being been so
widely diffused."   It is certainly true that the
lower classes are better off in some parts of the
United States than in Germany; America is the
wealthier country.   But there are a few points
which we must not overlook.   On the one hand,
well-being is a relative affair, more dependent
upon the changes in social life, whether up or
down, than upon the given status; and the
change upwards, the raising of the standard in
the last twenty years, is much more to be felt in
the fatherland than here; moreover, well-being
there is much less dependent upon wealth than
in the distinctly commercial atmosphere of this
country ; and the socialistically colored insurance
laws of Germany diminish the social hardships.
On the other hand, if the diffusion of American
wealth is accentuated, can it be denied that the
extremes are greater here than anywhere else, —
that the army of the unemployed is swelling while
the billion-dollar trusts are formed, that the rich-
est men are richer than any European, while the

slums of New York show a misery that is unknown in Berlin ?

A seventh reason for satisfaction with American democracy is "that no form of government ever inspired greater affection and loyalty." But can it be truly affirmed that the German nation feels less loyalty and affection for its constitutional monarchy, which does not appeal merely to the moral personality, but also to the æsthetic imagination? and does the affection for the form of government not fuse with loyalty for the highest representative of the nation? And yet, while the German is brought up from his childhood to loyal affection for the bearer of the crown, almost the half of the American population sees in the White House the man against whom their party effort was directed and whom they hope to fight again a few years hence.

There are no fewer grounds for questioning the eighth point of this presupposed superiority, " that nowhere has governmental power been more adequate to levy and collect taxes, to raise armies and to disband them, to maintain public order, and to pay off great public debts." But in what, in this respect, does the inferiority of the German government appear? Is it not usually conceded, even by the most fervent admirers of the democratic system, that the strong side of the European governments is their smooth working, due to the incomparable preponderance of experts and specialists? It has been asserted, again and again, that all the smooth effectiveness of expert government is morally less valuable than the rough working of a democratic machinery. Whether that is true is not the question now, but the assertion implies that at least the technique of government in America cannot be claimed as superior.

It has been maintained with full right that a further ground of the glory of American democracy — our ninth — is the way in which people of the most various races and nations have been absorbed by the vigorous organism of the United States. There is no doubt that no other country can show a similar achievement, but it is, at the same time, a fact that no other country has had the opportunity to try its skill in the solution of such a problem. The case of the immigrants who arrive on our shores with the full intention of becoming loyal Americans can scarcely be compared with that of the Polish or French or Danish population, which is unwillingly, and by the chance of history, amalgamated with the German nation. Those foreign elements which came by their own choice to Germany have been as thoroughly assimilated by the monarchy as the American immigrants by the democracy. America's whole success in that direction is determined by its geographical and economical situation, but not by its form of government.

The tenth point — it may be our last — is the noble progressiveness of the democratic nation. It has been said "that no people have ever welcomed so ardently new machinery and new inventions generally." But even if we consider progress merely from the narrow point of view of technique, it seems that Americans have fallen into certain misconceptions. Typical of these were the editorials of the press of the whole country when the report came that the United States' exhibition at the Paris World's Fair won the largest number of prizes. The triumph over Germany was at that time celebrated in all its variations. Only later came the commentary. The United States had, indeed, the largest number of awards, but, as the President of the American Manufacturers' Association declared, most of them were of secondary value, while the largest number of first prizes went to Germany. From the 121 groups into which the exhibition was divided, Germany triumphed in fifty-one, the United States in thirty-one, in spite of the fact that the number of German exhibits was only 2500, while those from the United States numbered 6564. On their incomparably broad scientific basis,

German industries, especially the chemical and electrical ones, have made the same rapid progress which American industries have enjoyed on the basis of greater wealth and commercial enterprise. In the same way the introduction of new inventions into the daily life has been not less characteristic of Germany. Moreover, progress means more than the production and introduction of machinery. Can it really be said that the genius of American democracy is more progressive than that of the German nation, if the word be taken in its broader sense? Does not the whole history of civilization show that the real decisive progress has always come from the great personalities, while it is characteristic of democracy to raise the average, but to keep down the great man? The democratic masses are progressive in the sense that if great men have opened a new way, they rush eagerly on; they want more and more of a given reform or of a given improvement, but to find a method of improvement or reform which is really new in principle is never their immediate concern; and yet that alone means progress from the standpoint of the world's history.

But this point in the discussion would lead us beyond our goal; our aim was at first not to criticise democracy, but merely to show that not every good thing in the United States can be

accredited to the existence of democracy. If it
be taken for granted that the love of peace,
religious toleration, the diffusion of education,
universal suffrage, the assimilation of foreign
elements, the safety of property, the love for the
government, the efficient working of the administration, the wide extension of well-being, and the
spirit of progress, — that all this because it is present in the United States is a product and characteristic of democracy, then any critical study of
the nature of democracy is superfluous. But such
an assumption would beg the question. We had
to ask, therefore, at the threshold of our inquiry,
whether monarchical Germany is inferior in these
points of distinction, and we have seen that the facts
speak against such an arbitrary hypothesis. The
value of democracy cannot be proved by reference
to qualities which are to the same degree, in some
respects perhaps even still more strongly, present
in a so-called aristocracy. It has thus been our
preparatory task to clear from the way of the discussion the popular notion that because America
is a glorious country under democratic government, therefore every American success must be
to the glory of democracy. With the same right,
the same reasons for satisfaction and pride might
be construed in Germany as arguments for the
superiority of the monarchical system. A fair

discussion will refuse such assistance and will consider the problem as a theoretical one.

II

A theoretical discussion of all sides of democracy was not our aim. We set out to answer the question of the American, whether the German ought not to prefer democracy. The question involves logically a full belief in the merits and advantages of democracy; the answer which has to explain why the German negatives the question is thus not bound to restate the arguments in favor of democratic government; they are considered as well known to the questioner, and the other side alone is in debate. No one, indeed, can be blind to the enormous moral advantages of democracy. It reinforces individual initiative, and through this the feeling of responsibility, it secures a high average of development, it stimulates every man to an equality of effort; and each one of these influences is worth being paid for in high sacrifices. Further, it makes an absolute change of policy possible, if the nation is dissatisfied with the old course; it reinforces the moral truth of the equality of men, and it avoids arbitrary and unjust standards of comparative valuation; in short, its ideal aim is moral, just, educative, and effective.

But have these merits not also their defects? is

the realization of these ideal ends probable or even possible? are not certain other ideals of equal value totally neglected? The German who seeks to inquire thus into the logical meaning and working of democracy may, of course, feel from the first disinclined to get his information from the United States, inasmuch as the experiment was made there under exceptionally favorable conditions. There was nothing typical in its development, and that unique combination of splendid possibilities might have made a noble showing, even if democracy had been the most deplorable form of government, and if everything had had to be achieved against the spirit of democracy. Here, in a land which, by its enormous possibilities, its abundant wealth, its freedom from traditions, attracted millions of the most energetic men of all nations, their combined efforts, not dissipated by the militarism which results from the geographical conditions of the European powers, must be effective in spite of any governmental scheme. To learn a lesson in comparative sociology the German, therefore, looks more naturally to France, where the periods of monarchy were not the least prosperous ones of the century; or to Brazil, where everything turned from good to bad when the régime of the old emperor was exchanged for a republic. But even if we take all our demonstrations of the practical results from the United States, how much power to convince belongs to those principles?

If we begin with the most seducing tenet of democracy, its belief in the equality of men and their equal right to determine the fate of the nation, we cannot doubt that the dangerous error of the appeal is hidden merely by the glittering generality of the term equality. That man is equal in so far as every one is equal before God is not a new doctrine; it did not have to wait for the state philosophers of the eighteenth century. Every man's good will has the same intrinsic, absolute value, but this moral truth does not involve any consequences as to the nature of man. The inequality of his strength and beauty, his talents and intellect, is more certain than his similarities; and power to determine by a logical decision the wisest course of national action is, of course, dependent upon his intellect, his insight, and his character; in short, dependent upon the unequal characteristics, and without any internal reference to the aspect in which man is really equal. The only excuse for political equality is thus not that it expresses the real equality, but that it is impartial to the different kinds of inequality. Every adjustment of political rights to the existing inequality of men is open to the reproach of unfairness and arbitrariness. If such adjustment were made according to educa-

tion, it would be easy to insist that the most educated are not necessarily the purest characters ;
if according to wealth or birth, it could be shown
that the rich man or the nobleman is not necessarily the most intelligent and the most educated.
Every system, in a word, involves some injustice,
and the only advantage of mechanical equality is
not that it is freer from injustice, but that it min-
gles all possible kinds of injustice, — without any
preference for a special one, indeed, but therefore,
also, without the possibility of securing at least
the partial justice of every other system. But
this small negative merit brings with it an abundance of defects and dangers, which must be
clearly felt by every unprejudiced observer of
American life. A by-product, visible on the surface, is the empty conventionality which finds its
ideal in likeness to one's neighbor. The constant
desire of the democratic American is to avoid an
individual standpoint, to accept a pattern in his
social and æsthetic and intellectual life, to dress
and to read, to travel and to talk like everybody
else. But the dogma of equality entrains much
greater evils. One is chronic dilettantism. In
a democratic community every one can do everything ; whether he is on a school board or in an
embassy, in a legislative or in an administrative
position, his guileless freedom from the influences

of technical preparation, together with the fact that he is a democratic citizen, fits him for the job. The need of specialized experts is not felt, and the result is an ineffective triviality which repels the best men and opens wide the door to dishonesty. The career of experts in all functions of public activity is the pride of Germany, — where the school committeeman or the mayor or the diplomat climbs up step by step, and reaches the greatest effectiveness by his lifelong specialization.

But worse even than democratic dilettantism is the lowness of aims which results from the belief in equality. If everybody's judgment is of equal value, only that is valuable which appeals equally to everybody. This is an indirect and yet a logically necessary consequence, which shows its practical results with an alarming clearness. There are only two good things which appeal to everybody, because they address the lowest instincts : money and physical strength. The result is that commercialism and athletics absorb the energies of men. That does not mean that those who hunt for wealth or indulge in sport do so in every case because their lower instincts are involved ; but it does mean that ends which appeal to the higher tendencies only remain ineffective as stimuli for the national life. The final outcome must be that commercialism, if left alone, would devastate

science and art, education and society, law and
politics ; city government and State legislature
would go over into the hands of men who cared
for the little money which was honestly in it, or
for the much money which was in it dishonestly,
and the national politics would become tainted by
the influence of commercial corporations.

But all this has also another side. Where the
belief in inequality somewhat discredits those premiums which appeal to the lower instincts, and
which are, therefore, desirable for every human
being, a certain outer organization of the national
life under the point of view of the aristocratic
values also becomes necessary. A kind of ideal
coin must be stamped which can circulate in daily
practical life like money ; a system of degrees, of
titles, of honors, of decorations must result which
give distinction without the power to satisfy the
lower instincts. They are based on examinations,
on creditable service, on the judgment of experts,
on excellence in all those directions where the appreciation of the masses stops. The consequences
are clear. The more this ideal coin gains credit,
the freer its owner becomes from the necessity of
appealing to the masses and of attracting the attention of the half-educated and the quarter-educated :
his title carries in a condensed form the appreciation of the experts. Where the democratic spirit

makes such coining impossible, man must appeal again and again to the masses, who have no memory and no refined discrimination. The result is not necessarily, as Europeans often wrongly imagine, a general mob-like vulgarity, but the more civilized forms of vulgarity : a bumptious oratory, a flippant superficiality of style, a lack of æsthetic refinement, an underestimation of the serious specialist and an overestimation of the unproductive popularizer, a constant exploitation of immature young men with loud newspaper voices and complete inability to appreciate the services of older men, a triumph of gossip, and a crushing defeat of all aims that work against the lazy liking for money-making and comfort. On the other hand, in an aristocratic country, the existence of a system of honors becomes secondarily a new form of appeal, even to the masses. As soon as people feel that the distinction of such honors given for intrinsic worth outweighs the distinction of wealth, the honors themselves become objects of desire, even for those to whom the ideal ends in themselves do not appeal. The development of a system of symbolic honors thus draws the people more and more away from commercialism and reinforces the striving towards higher aims and ideals. In its last results democracy must thus lower the aims of the best to the standard of

the masses, while aristocracy must push the masses
with their lower instincts into a striving towards
higher ends.

The foregoing stands in close relation to another feature of pure democracy, — the conspicuous absence of great men. Democratic leaders
are mostly men who take control of the movements of the masses, but not men who have the
inner greatness to lead the masses into new directions.   This is true for every field, for science and
literature, just as well as for internal and external politics.   The whole system must necessarily
push into the foreground the skillful manager
who appeals to the average man, and must keep
down the really great man, who goes the unpop-
ular way of new purposes.   No one can rise whose
working cannot be understood in every phase by
the man behind the plough.   And yet it is an
illusion to imagine that the great men can ever
be replaced by the high average of the masses.
A really great thought, a really great inspiration,
has never come from the diffused intelligence of
an aggregation or from the zeal of a multitude.
A parliament is an effective vehicle for acknowledged ideas, but it never gave rise to a new
thought; no philosophical or religious inspiration
ever came to the world by a majority vote.   The
democratic situation will make great work possi-

ble merely where this is the result of a gigantic coöperation, as demanded by commerce and industry, or where individual premiums in the form of great wealth stand as temptations, as in the case of practical inventions. It is not by chance that while American inventions are in line with the best inventions of Europe, they are none the less for the most part based on scientific discoveries made in Europe. Where coöperation is useless, as in every case of intellectual or æsthetical or moral effort, and where no commercial premium is offered, a democratic society must remain sterile and commonplace, since it has no means of stimulating the truly great men in their necessary solitude. Where a genius is needed, democracy appoints a committee.

Perhaps still more closely are defect and virtue bound together in the case of the democratic spirit of individual activity. Every one feels himself lawmaker and authority; the immediate result is the tendency to disregard every other authority but one's own self. A lack of reverence pervades the whole community and controls the family, the school, the public life. The pert American boy who does just what he pleases may thus get an early training in democratic politics; but while he wastes the best of the home and of the classroom, he gets at the same time the worst pos-

sible training for the duties of life, all of which
demand that he do later quite other things than
those which he likes to do.   He will learn too late
that it is a great thing to command, but a greater
thing to obey, and that no one can sign early
enough the declaration of dependence.   Where
no subordination is learned, no self-sacrifice and
no enthusiasm can be expected, and all institutions of the land must slowly adjust themselves
to the much-lamented influence of those who seek
merely pleasure and success.

But does not the individual independence in
democracy involve at least the highest degree
of liberty?   When Lecky, in his famous book,
coupled the two conceptions, his " Democracy and
Liberty " meant rather Democracy *versus* Liberty.   And Democracy remains the defendant
from whatever standpoint we may consider it.   If
we approach it from the side of social philosophy,
we must understand that, philosophically, freedom
means self-determination, but that self-determination is characterized not only by the absence of
outer determining factors, but by the harmonization of all the inner energies.   A man is not free,
in a moral sense, when he is a slave of his passions
and lower instincts, when he is unable to control
his impulses by his higher ideas.   In the same
way a social body gains no real liberty simply by

the overthrowing of external forces, but merely
by an organization in which the higher elements
control the lower ones, in which the representatives of social ideals supersede the forces of selfish
social instincts and vulgar impulses. A social
organism will thus be the more free, the more the
influence of the best men, of the noblest characters, and of the best educated personalities sup-
presses a system of equalization.

The outcome is the same if we come to the
question from a practical side. Democracy has,
first, a necessary tendency to abundant lawmaking
of a casuistic character, to restrictions and pro-
hibitions, and a continuous meddling with private
affairs, inasmuch as that is the only remedy for
evils at the disposal of such a community and the
only opportunity for the political representative
to prove his right to exist, not to mention some
reasons of less dignity. In democracies, more
easily than anywhere else, all kinds of protection
and prohibition interfere with the social and
economic liberties of the population. Further,
democracy, when it is not the question of a small
country, as in ancient Greece or in modern
Switzerland, but of scores of millions, must necessarily bring into existence the party machine, and
finally the party boss. That the machine and
boss system repels the best men from public life

and attracts the cheapest elements to politics, that it opens the doors for corruption and selfishness, is only one side of the shield; that it destroys civil liberty is the other. The rule of the machine is more tyrannical and more absolute than that of a king. The party rule in America, with its methods of nomination, deprives the individual of his political powers more completely than any aristocratic system, and the despotism of the boss easily turns into the tyranny of a group of capitalists. History has shown that this tyranny in democracy not seldom takes even the governmental form of a political dictatorship. That outcome is not to be feared in America, but simply because the American masses lack the æsthetic sense for the beauty of imperial pageantry, that sense which fascinates the French when Boulanger returns on his black horse from the parade. Democrats are always inclined to take bad æsthetical taste for good moral feeling.

Is the government of democracy at least an effective political instrument? Of course a government behind which the wealth and strength and power of a gigantic nation stand, is effective by its mere weight; but the question is whether it gains an additional advantage by the Democratic-Republican machinery. Has it, for instance, an advantage in political effectiveness over the

opposite extreme, — the government of Russia?
The Czar has had certainly no reason to be dissatisfied with the comparative success of his cabinet. To be sure, the democratic nation has this
great advantage, that the discontented majority
can break up the policy of the day and substitute
a new one; but in itself it is no improvement
simply to try the other party, and a state in which
all efforts at reform must necessarily take the
shape of seeking to throw overboard the existing
government, chooses, at least, a very indirect way
for the improvement of public affairs. In foreign
politics, too, the government naturally suffers in
several respects. It cannot have secrets ; it must
play all the time an open hand. It must make
continual concessions to public moods and caprices.
Further, it has not sufficient time at its disposal
to enter into far-reaching enterprises, as it cannot
rely on its own continuance. Nor can it, finally,
awaken in outsiders the confidence which an independent continuity of government engenders.

What do all the foregoing arguments prove?
Carthaginem esse delendam? That democracy
is an evil? Certainly not. We have emphasized
the great moral and educational and practical
achievements of the democratic spirit, and no
intelligent student of social philosophy can overlook the dangerous possibilities and the evil ten-

dencies of aristocratic society. The principles of equality and inequality are, then, both one-sided tendencies with immense energies and possibilities for good, but encompassed by dangers, both open to compromises with human selfishness and to demoralization by the masses or by the classes. The logical superiority of democracy is out of the question, and just as no American wishes to see Dewey or Roosevelt established as emperor, so no sane German wishes to see a political party leader become president of a German republic. What open-minded men on both sides wish can be merely that the unhealthy tendencies which are involved in each form of public life may be avoided and suppressed; but, in itself, the one state form does not stand higher than the other. The form of government under which a nation lives — so the educated average German would argue — depends upon the conditions of its historic development: a colony of men who went out as pioneers and who separated themselves from the mother country could not find unity and self-dependence under another form than that of the American democracy, while a land which hammers out its unity in welding a multitude of states, each with a long history under kings and princes, needs as its highest symbol the crown of an emperor.

If in these two lands everything were to be moulded by the form of the state alone, the final outcome would be the greatest possible difference in the national life of the two, — one thoroughly democratic, the other thoroughly aristocratic. But the other possibility is open, that each land supplements those tendencies which are a necessary consequence of its external form of public life by compensatory functions which reinforce the other side; if democracy counterbalances the evils of the crowd by social efforts of the aristocratic type, and if monarchy overcomes its intrinsic one-sidedness by democratic reforms and impulses, the differences will be unessential, and both countries will show a profound harmony of national instincts. Exactly that situation seems from day to day more the case of the United States and Germany. They become more and more alike, and the fact that one is by birth, and desires to remain, a monarchy, while the other desires to remain a republic, appears secondary and unessential. How is that possible? A hundred years ago the question of political government moved the world and determined the greatest differences. How has it become so unessential that no one to-day seriously considers the problem whether democracy or monarchy is the " better " form of state? And if the progress of history has abolished that problem, how does it happen that the new life in the two lands moves in opposite directions, — that on monarchical ground towards greater equality, that on democratic ground towards greater aristocracy, and both thus towards the same type of social existence, in spite of the important individual characteristics and differences?

To understand this whole situation we must take a more general point of view, perhaps even the most general one which the philosophy of history suggests.

III

If we try to bring order into the manifoldness of tendencies which characterize a period, we must seek the deeper motives and the underlying energies, as the mere classification of outer phenomena is easily misleading. For a newspaper editorial it may do, for instance, to call the nineteenth century the period of natural science, but the superficiality of such an appellation becomes clear to every one who examines more carefully the first half of the century, or, better, considers the progress of natural science and technique in periods that have gone before. When Schiller, one hundred years ago, praised the man of the eighteenth century, he called him the man who had mastered nature, and who was fascinated by the victory over the energies of nature. We cannot understand the times better if we choose another outer mark for the characterization of the time ; we must proceed from external to internal factors. It is so everywhere in scientific classifications. The child divides the animals into those of the air and those of the water, those of the air into such as fly and such as do not fly. The zoölogist neglects such external resemblances, and divides them into those with a backbone and those without a backbone ; and among the vertebrates, he distinguishes the mammals from the non-mammals, and so his classification separates much that seems to belong together. If we seek such principles of internal division for the phenomena of civilization, we find only one which is deep enough to allow us to comprehend the true connections : it is the division into realism and idealism. I know that some realist would at once be inclined here to think of the zoölogical classes we have just mentioned, and to consider the realists as beings with, and the idealists as beings without, a backbone. But we have at first not to praise and not to blame, but simply to separate the different types of human interests.

The realist seeks reality in objects, the idealist seeks it in ideas. The realist considers, therefore, that which is as final, and the idealist that which ought to be. The realist, therefore, relies on perception, the idealist on feeling. The one seeks to understand the world, the other to ennoble the world. The one works with the understanding, the other by means of inspiration. Realism, therefore, urges on to science, idealism to philosophy and religion ; and in the scientific realm the realist works inductively, the idealist deductively : the realist prefers natural science, the idealist historical science. The realist emphasizes technique, tries to master nature, and produces material for exchange ; the idealist finds his mission in art, masters nature by the inner liberation of his mind, and creates symbols. In art the realist is naturalist, the idealist comes in the garb of romanticism, of symbolism, or classicism. The realist seeks the essence of human life in pleasure and pain, the idealist in man's will. Therefore morality is, for the realist, based on utility : for the idealist, on the idea of good. For one the greatest happiness of the greatest number is the criterion, for the other the idea of duty, independent of happiness and majorities. As all men have equal capacities for pleasure and pain, the realist considers all men equal. The realist thus believes in the masses, the idealist in the hero and the genius. The realist is, therefore, democratic, the idealist aristo-

cratic : the realist is cosmopolitan and humanitarian, the idealist is national and imperialistic ;
the realist seeks his goal in liberty, the idealist in
justice.

Realism and Idealism are the two poles of mankind, and just as the realism of the man and the
idealism of the woman supplement each other in
every noble home, so these two great tendencies
have always coöperated in the history of the peoples. We have only to look to the two greatest
men of ancient Greece, the two men who controlled the thought of more than a thousand years,
Plato and Aristotle, to feel at once the typical expression of the two great tendencies. " Plato,"
says Goethe, " penetrates the world to fill it with
his own ideals ; he does not wish to analyze the
world, but to bring it into harmony with the good
and the true and the beautiful. Aristotle, however, approaches the world like a master builder ;
he examines the ground and brings material together and arranges it to build up his solid pyramid." As long as men will take a systematic
view of the world and of human life, it will be
ultimately Platonic or Aristotelian.

Such a coöperation of the two tendencies does
not mean simply their fusion, but rather their alternation ; and when they work together, — that
is, when they reach a compromise in a special case,

— a state of equilibrium ensues, and the problem is then relatively solved. But so long as there is to be development, the one or the other must prevail. As we cannot move towards the right and towards the left at the same time, so the social mind cannot turn, at the same time, to nationalism and cosmopolitanism, to naturalistic and to symbolistic art, to inductive and to philosophic science, to atheism and to religion. And such an alternation is the necessary outcome of the mental structure : every psychic movement has a tendency to go to an extreme, and the extreme has a tendency to produce a reaction in the opposite direction, which must itself go to the extreme again. If the tendencies alternate, it is clear that one alone does not mean progress and the other regress ; both are indispensable to development, and it is absurd to imagine that the realistic movement, for example, is alone progressive and the idealistic energy a hindrance to civilization. Whoever stands, in the battle of the day, on one side must see the enemy on the other side ; but from the standpoint of social philosophy, both energies, realism and idealism, are equally important and valuable. It is unfair to imply that realism is selfish and idealism unselfish : the utilitarian morality of the realist is not less unselfish than the intuitional morality of the idealist ; realism is not in its nature egoistic, just as idealism is not unpractical. And both sides can be equally inhuman and base. It was realism which sharpened the blade of the guillotine, and idealism which set fire to the funeral piles of the Middle Ages; it was realism which at times brought the mill laborers to the misery of starvation, and idealism which shot down the helpless lower races in the dark countries. Great and small men, clever and stupid men, noble and base men, have been always on either side.

If this alternation characterizes the progress of civilization, it is further clear that the movement cannot be a simple pendulum movement. The pendulum always swings again to the same point; civilization, on the other hand, moves forward. If civilization is realistic, then idealistic, then realistic again, it is not the same realism for a second time. The past is not simply repeated; the new movement arises from the same moral energies, but the whole foregoing development is included in the new position. Every phase of this gigantic counterplay brings certain problems to rest and fulfillment by a compromise, and new problems come to the front. Realism takes up one problem and carries its one-sided solution to an extreme; then awakes the idealistic countermovement and becomes powerful. Idealism takes

up new impulses and reinforces them till a realistic counter-movement begins ; but the first problem, since both sides have fought for it and have
defended their extreme positions, comes in the
mean time to a compromise, and thus ceases to be
a problem.   It is thus less a pendulum movement
than a spiral movement.   It is as if we should
climb up a tower by a spiral staircase ; we are
then looking from the windows of the tower, now
to the north and now to the south, but we never
look twice through the same window : whenever
the stair brings us back to the same side, the
window lies higher, the view has become more
extended.

Such alternations took centuries in the slow
rhythm of earlier civilization, but the changes
have come more and more swiftly, and in the last
hundred years they have followed each other with
the rapidity of generations, in so far as the great
fundamental movements of a world-civilization
are in question.   Of course, whenever one wave
begins to swell, it does not mean that the after-
effects of the foregoing wave have disappeared ;
while one world-tendency is at its maximum, the
movement of the last, and perhaps even of that
before the last, may still be felt, and the slow beginning of the next wave may already be percep-
tible to the sensitive mind.   And, secondly, this

great fundamental up and down of realism and idealism in the world's civilization does not exclude the possibility that the same change of realistic and idealistic energies may continue in narrower circles, in local realms, in special problems, independently of the great world-movements; a local realistic movement may thus coincide with a general realistic tendency, and thus reinforce it, or may fall together with a general idealistic wave, and thus inhibit it, or limit it to certain regions.

This change from generation to generation is reflected very clearly in the alternating phases of philosophical thought. The middle of the eighteenth century was controlled by a realistic view of the world: experience and analysis were the methods — sensualism, skepticism, materialism were the results; the spirits of Locke and Hume, of the French encyclopædists and Voltaire, were in the foreground. The reaction came with the German idealism of the end of the eighteenth century; Kant emphasizes the " ought " as against the " is," and the idealistic philosophy, in its increasing energy from Kant to Fichte, to Schelling, and finally to Hegel, conquers the philosophical world. Hegelianism represents the extreme which demands a realistic reaction; before the middle of the nineteenth century is reached, idealism lies again in the dust, a new realism triumphs, positivism and materialism push to the foreground, Comte and Spencer become the spokesmen of an unphilosophic age, and natural science, with Darwin and Helmholtz as leaders, absorbs the philosophizing interest of the time. But before the nineteenth century came to an end, the situation changed once more : for about ten years philosophy has been again on the idealistic track. While realistic philosophy ran to its extreme, from materialism to psychologism and sociologism, a serious idealistic reaction began in the midst of empirical scientists who had despised philosophy for forty years. The leading thinkers, the world over, plunged again into epistemological inquiries, Kant and Fichte were revived, and an ethical voluntarism grew from year to year. The situation of the world's scholarship of to-day shows decidedly in every line the philosophical, idealistic trend, notwithstanding that it has found so far no overwhelming classic expression : the wave is only swelling to-day, its highest point may be ten or twenty years hence. This up and down of realism and idealism in philosophical thought is not a chance feature, nor even a by-product of civilization, but the clearest expression, and perhaps most central factor, of the world's development throughout that period. The French philosophy of the eighteenth century cannot be separated from the

French Revolution or from the American Declaration of Independence. The anti-idealistic movement of the post-Hegelian time, with its overestimation of the natural sciences, cannot be separated from the development of modern industry and modern technique. And thus in every way the philosophical movements were both the moving powers and the indicators of the whole rhythm of civilization. The Western civilization, as a whole, shows, indeed, a realistic character in the second half of the eighteenth century, an idealistic wave in the first third of the nineteenth, a new realism since the middle of it, and the beginning of a new idealism near the close of the nineteenth century. We might just as well have followed it in the movements of art and literature. Can it be doubted that the realistic period of naturalism in art is over, and that, since the days of the new symbolism, a young idealism is passing through the art exhibitions of all countries? or that the period of Zola's realism is a thing of the past, and that Ibsen and Tolstoy and Hauptmann and Kipling approach, from very different quarters, the realm of idealism? or can we overlook the corresponding alternation between realistic cosmopolitanism and idealistic nationalism, and, nearly connected therewith, the alternating phases of human belief in the equality and in the inequality of men? The former breaks the chains of the slaves, the latter takes up the burden of the white man. Our own period, as it presses towards philosophy and religion in its thought and towards idealism in its art, must be nationalistic and expansionistic.

But the strongest feature of this movement of the last hundred and fifty years has not been pointed out so far. The realism of the eighteenth century was first of all democratic, the reaction in the nineteenth was necessarily aristocratic, monarchic, imperialistic : the outcome was a compromise, for Europe the constitutional monarchy ; and by this compromise, as always happens, the movement itself came to an end, the problem ceased to exist. In the second half of the nineteenth century the form of political government was no longer a question which moved peoples. How far otherwise was it considered in the eighteenth, and how narrowly connected with all the other phases of the realistic movement, with its philosophy and its religion, its literature and its social life ! It was the great period of enlightenment, which worked with sober clearness, with skeptical understanding, with humanitarian common-sense. Such a period must have one aim above all, not to allow any illusions. And as the foregoing idealistic period had left a world full of

illusions and symbols of a religious and historical
character, the chief energy of the time had to become destructive, and to turn against the authority
of the church and of the state : equality and liberty sounded in all the streets. It was a period
rich in its inheritance for the following century,
full of humanitarian and civil impulses, and yet it
was narrow and Philistine, as is every enlightenment of the understanding alone : it was anti-his-
torical, anti-religious, anti-artistic, with no imagination, no emotion, no great historical consciousness ;
and the idealistic reaction was unavoidable. The
time of Hegel and Goethe and Beethoven had to
be the time of Napoleon and of Prussia's war for
its national independence ; it was the time when
romanticism and Gothic art awoke again, and
mankind thought more of the genius than of the
masses. The fusion of these two great antagonistic tendencies eliminated this problem.

When the great reaction against romanticism
came, it could not again be a return to the standpoint of the eighteenth century, but it brought
new problems forward as the old ones had reached
a compromise. The new problems came from the
new realism, which meant natural science, modern
industry and commerce and transport and medicine. But here, again, the movement had to work
itself to an end, to reach an extreme which de-

mands reaction.   We stand in the middle of it.
The new discoveries are no longer solutions of
life-problems, but luxuries ; the phonograph is
not what the telegraph was.   Above all, modern
industry brought up the question of modern labor,
the social conscience awoke, a new type of man,
the mill laborer, stood before the world ; and mankind recognized that he was helpless, and must
become daily more helpless, in the presence of
combined capital.   The idealistic reaction began,
the social question absorbed the thinking world,
and thus the great antagonism of energies, of the
same mental energies which fought a hundred
years ago over the problems of state form, are
concentrated to-day on the problems of the social
question.   The idealistic reaction in which we live
will grow to a point where a compromise will be
reached, and the social problem will then become
as obsolete and indifferent as the political problem
of monarchy or republic is to-day ; and while the
alternation of idealism and realism will go on,
new and ever new problems will offer themselves
as the results of the new fields which are opened
up by these antagonistic energies.

IV

We have answered our first question, how it
has come about that the question of monarchy or
republic has been laid on the table in the congress
of nations ; but we have not answered the second
question, why the republic of America and the
monarchy of Germany approach each other by
a movement in opposite directions,—the United States moving towards aristocracy, Germany
towards democracy. But the foregoing reduction
of all human efforts to the alternation of realistic
and idealistic energies contains, also, the explanation of this second phenomenon. We emphasized
from the first that the great progress of general
civilization of the whole Western world is not the
only illustration of that counterplay of energies :
the world-movements are accompanied by local
movements of far-reaching independence. The
French Revolution, Darwinism, electro-technique,
and the labor question are world-movements which
cannot be localized ; but other waves are limited
by the boundaries of a nation, others even by the
walls of a town or of a set or of a group : any
social unit may have its independent alternation of
realistic and idealistic energies. While the general
world-movements show to-day the ebbing of a great
realistic wave, which was at flood tide twenty years

ago, and the slow upward swelling of an idealistic wave, which has not yet broken, there is a local realistic democratic movement just now sweeping over Germany and an idealistic tendency over the United States. Both are determined by local conditions, but both work towards a surprising similarity of the two forms of national life, inasmuch as they are necessarily diminishing those differences which resulted from the different forms of the historical constitution.

It may sound paradoxical, and yet it can hardly be doubted that, within a certain limit, it is on both sides the same cause which has had an opposite effect. It is the accumulation of wealth which creates the aristocratic movement in America and which spreads a democratic spirit over Germany. The strenuous pioneer life, where wealth begins merely in the first generation, has no room for class discrimination and for aristocratic fashion, culture, art, and taste; on the other side, in the society in which the nobleman is the rich landowner and high officer and state official, with all the power in his traditional rights, while the population is poor, and therefore powerless, there is no chance for democratic ideas. But if inherited wealth and a leisure class grow up on the one side of the ocean, and if commerce and industry bring wealth to the middle classes on the other side, then the time for a change has come.

Two recent novels, one American and the other German, throw light on the contrasts of the situation. "In this country we are all free and equal," says Selma in Robert Grant's "Unleavened Bread," and Flossie retorts, "Yes, there is something of the sort in the Declaration of Independence, but that was put in as a bluff to console salesladies. . . . People here are either in society or out of it, and society itself is divided into sets. There's the conservative aristocratic set, the smart rapid set, the set which has not much money, but has Knickerbocker or other highly respectable ancestors, the new millionaire set, the literary set, the intellectual philanthropic set, and so on. . . . Most of the people in these different sets are somebodies because either their grandfathers or they have done something well — better than other people — and made money as a consequence. And when a family has made money or won distinction by its brains, and then has brushed its teeth twice a day for two generations, the members of it, even though dull, are entitled to respect, don't you think so?"

And now as a contrast to Grant's ironical sketch, so full of truth, let me quote the splendid novel of Georg von Ompteda, — "Eysen." It is the life portrait of the family von Eysen, an old noble family which has belonged for centuries to

the aristocratic set which has controlled social life
by holding the high positions in state and army
and owning the great country estates. It now
sees that a new time is coming, and feels that the
land is passing into the hands of the new mer-
chants and bankers and industrials and that
the higher standard of the middle classes, with
their hard work and intellectual energy, is bringing them more and more to power and leadership.
The General von Eysen is conscious that he has
overcome his old prejudices : he has given permission to his only son to become neither officer
nor state official, but engineer ; and at a reunion
in which he meets the younger members of his
family he says in his toast : " Above all — you
must work ; who does not work, must sink. Be
everywhere — not only where we could be found
in the past — on our own ground, in the state
service, in the army. . . . We live in a new time
and a new time demands new conditions; give
honor to the tradition, but do not become its
slaves. If you look only backward to the history
of the past, you will lose your freedom. . . . No,
my young relatives, we old families do not want
to be submerged. Go into art, into science and
medicine, sit on the merchant's stool, guide your
ships into foreign seas for the honor and advantage of the German name ; enter life not only as

state officers, but as lawyers, or as architects;
wherever in the world money is to be gained by
the exertion of commerce and industry, go and
take part; money in the right hand gives freedom."

Yes, a new time has come for Germany; in
thirty years of undisturbed peace it has grown
rich, it has changed from an agricultural country
into an industrial country, the standard of life
has been raised with an undreamed of rapidity,
the horizon has been widened, the new industry
has pushed trade over the ocean, a colonial system
has grown up, and all has had only one effect in
common, — the rise of the democratic spirit in
the noblest meaning of the word. It has not
taken anything from the aristocratic power of the
empire, has not touched all the noble achievements of an aristocratic army and state service,
has even reinforced the German's love for his king
and his princes; and yet, as General von Eysen
said, the new time has come. The symptoms are
felt wherever we turn. The raising of the social
level of the business man, the merchant, and the
industrial man, together with the sinking of the
social level of the landowner, is certainly one of
the most prominent features. The power which
the great representatives of industry and commerce and banking and the market have to-day

in the state organism of Germany could not have been dreamt of twenty years ago, and the number of high officials who seek business positions grows rapidly. There is a certain analogy in the steady raising of the practical professions, that of the engineer and the scientist, in comparison with the literary professions ; the entire education is being turned, and not least through the Emperor's influence, in the direction of practical, technical achievements as over against the classic traditions. It is the same principle which emancipates the woman, a movement which, after a long time of waiting, to-day perhaps overhastens its progress : the democratic desire for equality must demand the same rights for women. But the principle of emancipation applied to the business world, the practical professions, the women, cannot be limited to the middle classes; the same tendency must help the lower classes also. Nowhere, perhaps, does the " new time " appear more clearly. The social-democratic party, which was, even ten years ago, considered and suppressed as an enemy of the state, becomes daily more and more a coöperating member of the social organism, while the material fate of the laborer is protected by the state socialism, which has become law. And, above all, the intellectual and æsthetic interests of the masses are growing with the higher standard of the whole population. The reading of papers, the formation of clubs and societies, discussions and lectures, reach wider and wider circles, while rich men begin, in growing measure, to devote large gifts to public benefits. Add thereto the new enthusiasm for the sea, for naval affairs, for foreign lands beyond the ocean, a widening of the horizon which necessarily has a democratic tendency, and which greatly reinforces the spirit of independence and individual activity ; add the immense development of technique, of transportation, of means of communication, all thoroughly democratic factors, since they put men more on an equal footing and bring progress within the reach of every one ; add the whole increase of the yearly saving, which means better food and better houses, health and cleanliness and enjoyment, — and if we sought to compress all into one word, we might say, Germany has become in the last ten years Americanized. The thoroughly aristocratic nation, with all its appreciation for the historical forces and symbols, for arts and education, for the leadership of the educated, and for the acknowledgment of authority, has added to itself since the coming of the new time the individual activity and the equality of the ideal democracy.

And America ? Is Flossie right, — has equality

become only a bluff for the consolation of salesladies? Certainly not! Democracy is still to-day
the rock on which the United States is built, and
will remain so, exactly as Germany in its deepest
structure will remain monarchical; and yet, if it
is true that Germany becomes democratic, in a
thousand respects it is still more true that America becomes aristocratic : a new time has come for
America, too. Of course I do not have in mind
here those pseudo-aristocratic and pseudo-mon-
archic tendencies which work against the democratic institutions by dishonest means and intolerable abuses : bossism is merely the caricature of
aristocracy ; and while it is true that Quay and
Croker and their likes are tyrants without a constitutional background, whose whims lead men on
to fortune or destroy them, this tyranny is the
outgrowth of democracy and not at all the legacy
of aristocratic impulses.

But even when we turn to the really aristocratic symptoms of national life, the question is not
whether we welcome or deprecate them ; we are
interested merely in the question whether the phenomena exist. Thus it cannot be our task here
to inquire whether the United States is wise or
unwise in its policy of aggressive expansion,
whether it would be better to remain loyal to the
principles of the past, which reduced the chances

of friction with other nations, and thus saved to the land the burdens of militarism, or whether the progress of the country demands that new responsibilities be courageously faced. For us it is sufficient that imperialism is a symptom of the aristocratic attitude towards man, and that imperialism is the creed of the country. Imperialism means the belief in the inequality of men, which, as we emphasized from the beginning, follows the logic of idealism. It is true that only one of the two great parties stood for the imperialistic policy in the last presidential election ; but the social psychologist cannot doubt that the Democrats were anti-imperialistic only because the Republicans had chosen otherwise beforehand ; while the Democratic masses, before the campaign had hammered the issue into their minds, were not less carried away by the Kipling mood than the other half of the nation. But it was not even necessary to wait till the Philippine issue was brought before the American consciousness. The suppression of the Chinese in California, the barriers erected against the undesirable types of immigrants from Europe, above all, the adroit laws to deprive the negro of his vote, — all speak the same language, all demonstrate the same way of feeling : the aristocratic morality of a powerful and noble nation, what Nietzsche called the morals of mas-

ters — so different from the democratic morals of
slaves, who try to make the world believe that all
men are equal.

But does this undemocratic spirit turn against
the outsider only? Where is the equality in the
inner life of America? Of course it is true that
we have public schools where all are equal; the
only difficulty is that they are not in use. Yes,
there is no doubt that we are fast approaching a
state where nobody in a city sends his children to
the public schools when his means allow him to
pay for the instruction of a private school. "Tout
comme chez nous!" The whole educational system is rapidly becoming aristocratic. This case
is similar to that of travel by rail. Americans
who go to Europe like to ridicule the class differences in the European trains and boast that American railroads have only one class; but on inquiry
it appears that it is hard to find any one of your
acquaintance who travels in America, from one
large city to another, without carefully avoiding
that single class by sitting in the parlor car. And
this exclusiveness of the passenger reflects the
character of society. The plan after which the
smart set, and not in New York and Newport
alone, celebrates its festivities and weds its brides
is not only the pattern of fashion and luxury, but
a conscious imitation of aristocracy. A typical

expression is found in the immense growth of the
pedigree craze. The marriages of American heir-
esses with European fortune hunters of the nobility seem to me un-American, and thus not typical :
it is the fancy of individuals and not a symptom
of national life. But the genealogical passion,
" the pedigree spleen," grows out of the best material of the nation, and yet it is thoroughly anti-
democratic. If a single family of Connecticut
needs three volumes of 2740 quarto pages to
print its own history; if the Daughters of the
Revolution have 27,000 members; if the genealogical societies like the Colonial Dames, the
Daughters of the Holland Dames, the Mayflower
Descendants, and so on, multiply with every year,
— the aristocratic undercurrent cannot be doubted.
It is thus not by chance that the old Southern
aristocracy just now begins to become somewhat
reconciled : public life begins to move more and
more in their direction.

And all this is reflected in the public life. We
know the simplicity, according to the tradition at
least, with which that President of the past went
on horseback alone to the Capitol to take the oath
of office, and tied his horse to the post; we know
the military pageantry which accompanied the
last presidential inauguration. And this aristocratic desire for the outer symbolic decoration

percolates through all layers of society, down to the car conductor and the elevator boy, who are proud of their distinguishing uniform, while, only a short time ago, as I am informed, a free American still objected to wearing any uniform in civil life. The tendency to develop more refined and polished manners belongs necessarily to the change; the spitting and chewing decrease from year to year, and the men who put their feet on the table and the women who rock while they are talking become rarer specimens.

But these are matters of external life. It is the inner vitality in which the really important changes are felt, changes which are essentially beyond difference of opinion, changes which cannot be disposed of as snobbish, and which none the less are decidedly aristocratic. Here belongs the steadily increasing influence of college-bred men in public life; the fact itself has recently been often demonstrated with full statistics, and its meaning is clear : the men of superior education are brought to that superior position which aristocracy willingly offers them, and which democracy finally cannot deny them, in spite of the flagrant inconsistency of the act. Parallel with this movement there necessarily goes a twofold development : the growth of the feeling of public duties and responsibilities and the substitution of æsthetic and intellectual ideals for those of a merely commercial character.

There will, of course, always be pessimists who lament that the present is worse than the past ; and for editorials with a point against Tammany or against Wall Street, it is the right thing to begin by declaiming that politics has reached its lowest moral ebb, or that the whole life of the land is sacrificed to commercialism. This may be effective, but it is not true. The stronger current of the nation is at present setting in the opposite direction. The number of men who, unselfishly and with high ideals, serve the community in a thousand forms is undoubtedly increasing every day. The Roosevelt type is increasing in politics, but far more outside of politics. If the feeling of duty led merely to financial bequests, it ought not to count for too much in a country in which — compared with Germany, for instance — the rich men pay so small a tax ; but those men should count who give their time and effort, their intellect and honesty, to public trusts. " Noblesse oblige " is daily more felt ; but it presupposes, of course, the " noblesse," the aristocracy. That the new time means a new life for art and science must impress every one. The rapid growth of our graduate schools, with their goals far beyond the reach of the college, demands an understand-

ing of the value of pure knowledge, which offers itself at first only as a luxury of the leisure classes :
truth for truth's sake belongs to an aristocratic
society. And since the days of the Chicago
Fair and the Washington and Boston libraries,
the wave of American art is swelling. All the
conditions are surely favorable to it. History
has always shown that art comes to fullest flower
whenever wealth is abundant, so that a leisure
class may exist, and when, at the same time, a
characteristic national development arises. The
leisure class is as yet made up for the most part
of women, but the more wealth comes into the
second and third generation, the more men are
joining their ranks. And the more the new politics brings the country into relations with other
nations, the more it becomes conscious of the spe-
cific national characteristics of its civilization.
This beautifying impulse, which is so strictly antagonistic to the utilitarian aspect of democracy,
brightens the whole country. Ten years ago the
railroads were no less well equipped, but the railroad stations were painful to a European eye ; the
new stations built in the last ten years in the leading cities reflect the whole development of a nation which is passing through an aristocratic period.
Not the narrowness of the farmer, but the æsthetic
taste of the educated controls the outer forms of

public life, and the marble of the public halls teaches the masses that they must refine their manners. Still more evident is a growing refinement in the industrial arts and in the decoration of the home. Democratic wealth admires silverware and jewelry; aristocratic life does not care for the value of the material, but appreciates the form, the idea, the soul : Tiffany glass and Rookwood pottery would have been impossible in America twenty years ago.

One other position democracy begins slowly, too slowly, to surrender : the democratic belief that everybody can do everything, if he only will, is slowly fading, and the public, not less than every corporation, demands expert talent for its business, with the necessary changes on all sides. It demands, first of all, civil service reform and a pension system. The pension system, outside of the army, is undemocratic, and thus foreign to the United States till recent years ; it is one of the greatest blessings of the aristocratic wave that it carries the pension system into the most different fields of life, and thus creates the repose of faithful service which knows itself protected and is not obliged to push itself constantly before the attention of the masses. Even in the highest classes of service, like university work, the pension idea is only five years old. On the other hand, there are symptoms that the salary question, also, in all walks of public life, will be settled in the near future. To-day the judges of the Supreme Court, the Vice-President, the members of the Cabinet, and correspondingly all the lower offi-cials, are paid according to the naïve democratic idea that the salary must be large enough so that some one who is ready to take the job can be found for it. This farmer's economy is disap-pearing, and the public is learning an aristocratic lesson from the big trusts and corporations. This undemocratic belief in the authority of the ex-pert brings the regular army steadily forward in public estimation, while the volunteers are losing ground. The demand for a diplomatic career, for a systematic schooling for consular and diplo-matic service, daily becomes louder ; the time for democratic dilettantism has gone ; since America has become a world-power, it has too much to lose. The government cannot play any longer with a hand always open to the criticism of every editorial writer, and its diplomats need the pre-paration of a lifetime ; in short, America daily becomes more like the others, and among the "others" especially like Germany, where the be-lief in the superiority of expert work and expert judgment has found its fullest development and realization.

Germany is Americanizing and America is Germanizing, and nothing at this stage can stop the further development in that direction ; it has become necessary as an outlet for energies which were artificially kept down by aristocracy in Germany and by democracy in America. Only since these two national movements have supplemented the existing tendencies, are both countries fully prepared for their rôles as leaders on the globe. Germany will remain a monarchy, America a republic and democracy in its entire political structure, and yet this political difference will be daily less felt, because, as we have seen, the political questions of the state forms have lost their character as problems. They have not lost their importance, but they have, like morality, become a matter of course, which is not under discussion, and which must be understood from historical conditions ; the constitutional difference no longer means any difference of opinion. The " problem " has become a social one, and it is just this field in which, as we have seen, the development of the last years has brought about in both countries the same result. The same end-point, a complete harmonization of aristocratic and democratic energies, has been reached from two opposite starting points. There is no third country for which that is equally true. It points to the profound similarity between the Americans and the Germans, a similarity which was a long time hidden by the dissimilarity of occupations. Now, however, that the pioneer period of America is over and that Germany is entering into the world-market, the time has come when the deep harmony of their natures can fully show itself. This kinship of character is the best security for a future of lasting peace, not free from competition and rivalry in all fields of commerce and industry, of science and art, of culture and ideals, but free from animosity and ill will. Whatever fate may bring, the present conjunction of the stars would seem to betoken that Americans and Germans will never again forget that they belong together.

The Riverside Press

Electrotyped and printed by H. O. Houghton & Co.

Cambridge, Mass., U. S. A.

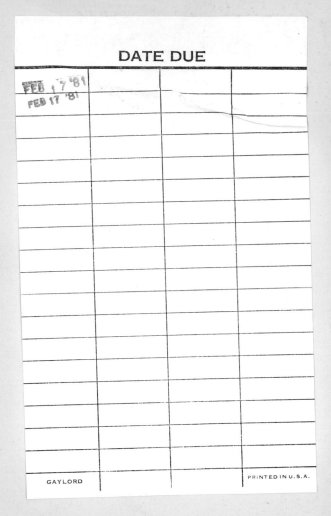

DATE DUE

FEB 17 '81			
FEB 17 '81			
GAYLORD			PRINTED IN U.S.A.